a daughter's worth

a bible study for teenaged girls

by

Ava H. Sturgeon

Tate Publishing, LLC.

"A Daughter's Worth" by Ava H. Sturgeon

Copyright © 2006 by Ava H. Sturgeon. All rights reserved.

Published in the United States of America
by Tate Publishing, LLC
127 East Trade Center Terrace
Mustang, OK 73064
(888) 361–9473

Book design copyright © 2006 by Tate Publishing, LLC. All rights reserved.

No part of this publication may be reproduced, stored in a retrieval system or transmitted in any way by any means, electronic, mechanical, photocopy, recording or otherwise without the prior permission of the author except as provided by USA copyright law.

All scripture quotations are taken from the Holy Bible, New International Version ®, Copyright © 1973, 1978, 1984 by International Bible Society. Used by permission of Zondervan Publishing House. All rights reserved.

ISBN: 1–5988639–8-3

dedication

for courtney, olivia, and samantha, the
next generation of worthy daughters.

acknowledgment

God gave me a tender heart for teenaged girls, and so this labor of love
was written just for them. The project, years in the making, gradually
evolved into a community effort: Grandma Grace Hoomes, whose prayers
sustained me; my mom, Lucky Hoomes, who is my biggest cheerleader;
my dad, Buck Hoomes, who trusted in God's timing; Bill, an incredibly patient husband, who encouraged me daily; my sister, Andrea Baker,
who helped me navigate my first writer's conference; employer Frank
Lay, who granted personal leave for this endeavor; youth director Den-
nis Dean, who permitted me to teach this study before it was published;
fifteen teenaged girls at Olive Baptist, who inspired me each Monday
night, and my Lord Jesus Christ, who indeed offers life abundant.

table of contents

foreword

In *A Daughter's Worth,* Ava Sturgeon has created a life-experienced, classroom-tested Bible study with real appeal for today's young ladies. One glance at the Table of Contents verifies she understands the issues we females face (no matter our ages!). Her passion for challenging the spiritual lives of teenagers is projected on every page.

The concise, easy-to-use text provides guidance to all girls who wish to pursue lives pleasing to God. Readers are encouraged to study Scripture, contemplate life application, and enrich their prayer lives by spending time daily with their Heavenly Father.

Oh, how beneficial this valuable resource would have been forty years ago when I was a teen! I needed Ava's assurance and confident hope that I would survive life, love, family and friendship and make it to the ripe old age of twenty.

Liz Traylor
Teacher, writer, speaker
Pastor's wife, Olive Baptist Church
Pensacola, Florida

introduction

A Daughter's Worth is a twelve-week, interactive Bible study for teenaged girls, written in a fresh, approachable way without ever backing down from God's truth. Each topic deals frankly with modern struggles, many of them uniquely female: realizing self-worth; dealing with emotions; dating with confidence, and handling the pressures of comparison. The study also focuses on universal concerns, such as finding good friends; living peacefully with family; sharing beliefs, and following God's direction.

Although teens can certainly use this book for individual reflection, a group study enables them to share thoughts and gain insight from an adult leader. Before gathering each week to discuss a specific topic, teens complete five brief devotions which include scripture, contemporary examples, journaling, and prayer. At the conclusion of each devotion, additional prompts encourage them to dig deeper.

When the study is complete, teenaged girls embrace the privileges and responsibilities of being God's child. At the same time, they've practiced the discipline of daily Bible study, prayer, and application. Most of all, *A Daughter's Worth* reinforces the timeless wisdom of God's word, regardless of gender, age, or circumstance.

week 1

overview

recognizing your worth

Let's face it: Being a teenager in the 21st century is tough. But growing up as a Christian young woman is even tougher, especially when you're searching for God in a world that often ignores Him. Would you like to experience God's undeniable presence in your day-to-day life? Check any areas in which you could use some divine intervention:

____ Feeling better about myself   ____ Dealing with friends and boyfriends

____ Getting along with family   ____ Making plans for the future

____ Handling stress at school

understanding my purpose

If you're a child of God, then here's some wonderful news: Regardless of the world's attempts to push Him out, your Heavenly Father is as involved and powerful as ever, just waiting to show you the happiness He offers. Read David's prayer to God in Psalm 106:4–5: *Remember me, O Lord, when you show favor to your people, come to my aid when you save them, that I may enjoy the prosperity of your chosen ones, that I may share in the joy of your nation and join your inheritance in giving praise.*

1. If you're a chosen daughter of God, then which five benefits do you receive from the Father?

a) God shows _____ to you, His daughter.

b) God comes to your _____ when you need help.

c) God wants you to enjoy_____ .

d) God wants you to share in the _____ of the Heavenly family.

e) God wants you to join (and benefit from) His amazing

_____ .

2. If you're a chosen daughter of God, then why is it so difficult to apply these benefits to your everyday life?

_____

_____

_____

There's no denying that everywhere you go, society threatens your self-esteem, your future, and your very identity as God's child. Can you successfully combat these dangers and live in victory? Absolutely! The first step is understanding who you are and why you're special. Read Romans 5:6–8 in your Bible. How do you know for sure that your worth, according to God, is priceless?

_____

_____

_____

Your Heavenly Father has already determined that you're worth the ultimate sacrifice. Now He wants to reveal His powerful presence in every aspect of your life. No matter what the world suggests, your life as a teenager can be happy, fulfilling, and yes, Godly.

That's what this Bible study is all about: embracing your worth as a daughter of God and using it to change the world around you, one day at a time. Please, hang in there for the entire study, and watch God transform your self-esteem, your standards, and your purpose. Once you understand the benefits and responsibilities of your worthy heritage, the opportunities are endless!

what to do next . . .

Are you ready to discover your priceless worth as a daughter of God? For each daily devotion, you'll need your Bible, study book, pen or pencil (yes, you'll be writing in your book), highlighter and a quiet place.

Starting tomorrow, you'll spend just 10–15 minutes completing the first devotion of Week 2. Then the next day, you'll read the second devotion, and so on until all five days have been completed. Try to read one a day rather than cramming several devotions into one time frame: That way, you'll be thinking about the topics throughout the entire week. When your study group meets to discuss the topics for Week 2, you'll be ready to share your thoughts.

I'm so happy that you're open to God's life-changing truth. I've witnessed exciting growth in teenagers just like you who recently completed this same study. I'll be praying for you!

week 2

accepting the Father's love

Do you realize that when you decide to follow Christ, you become a cherished daughter? The minute you are born into the Heavenly family, amazing advantages are at your fingertips. Are you making the most of these privileges? This week, we'll look at some of the perks of being a worthy daughter of God.

> *"I will be a Father to you and you will be my . . . daughters," says the Lord Almighty.* 2 Corinthians 6:18

day 1: your Father wanted you to be born.

Not everyone is lucky enough to be raised by a loving, earthly father. Many girls today don't know their biological fathers at all. Still others don't see their dads very often. There's good news, though, for every daughter who longs to be "daddy's girl." The Heavenly Father, filled with unimaginable love, holds you close and celebrates your every breath. Read these two verses from Isaiah:

This is what the Lord says— "He who made you, who formed you in the womb, and who will help you: Do not be afraid. . . ." Isaiah 44:2

Now, this is what the Lord says— "He who created you . . . Fear not, for I have redeemed you; I have summoned you by name; you are mine." Isaiah 43:1

1. How do you know for sure that God planned your birth?

_____

_____

_____

2. How do you know for sure that God will take care of you?

_____

_____

_____

Regardless of your experience with an earthly father, the Creator proudly proclaims, "You are mine." He promises to stick around because He chose you, and He enjoys your existence. Read 1 Peter 2:9 in your Bible. What happens after you've been chosen?

_____

_____

_____

Ladies, you are chosen; you are loved; you are holy, and you belong to God, the dependable and loving Father. He wants a life for you that's full of promise. Spend some time thanking your Heavenly Father for life, for choosing you, and for providing the way to become a worthy daughter.

one more thing . . .

Read Ephesians 1:4, and then summarize it here.

_____

_____

_____

_____

_____

_____

_____

_____

_____

_____

_____

_____

_____

_____

_____

_____

_____

_____

_____

_____

_____

_____

_____

_____

_____

_____

_____

day 2: your Father delights in your existence.

Have you ever noticed young parents when their toddler discovers something new? Whether it's finding a dandelion or throwing a ball, that child's accomplishment is celebrated by her proud mom or dad. Your Heavenly Father feels the same way when you enjoy the gift of life. To put it simply, you are a delight to God!

Read Zephaniah 3:17: *The Lord your God is with you; He is mighty to save. He will take great delight in you; He will quiet you with His love; He will rejoice over you with singing.*

1. Circle the phrases in the verse that show God's delight in knowing you.
2. Why do you think that God enjoys knowing you specifically?

_____

_____

_____

Realizing God's delight in your existence is a wonderful ego booster. Your Creator, the Father of *everything,* is always happy to hang out with you. Thank the Lord now for all the ways He brings you joy, and then list some of them here:

_____

_____

_____

Because God delights in His daughters, you can approach Him with any concern, no matter how trivial. He simply wants to spend some time with you. What does Ephesians 3:12 say about approaching God in prayer?

_____

_____

_____

Ladies, there's no reason to hold back when you're talking with God. He not only loves you more than any earthly parent, but He also enjoys being your Father. He gets a kick out of you: that strange sense of humor, your warm smile, and your amazing potential. After all, He made you. Tell God what's on your heart—He'd love to hear it, straight from your lips.

one more thing . . .

God delights in you, but do you enjoy spending time with God? Read Psalm 116 aloud and write a similar prayer of thanks for the gift of pure delight.

_____

_____

_____

_____

_____

_____

_____

_____

_____

_____

_____

_____

_____

_____

_____

_____

_____

_____

_____

_____

_____

_____

_____

_____

day 3: your Father protects you.

I always wanted an older brother, a protective guy who would watch out for me in school. He would stand up to bullies, question my boyfriends, and keep me out of trouble. What I got instead was a younger brother who frankly showed no interest in his older sister. Thankfully, though, I have a Heavenly protector who never lets me down. I hope that He's your Father, too.

What scares you? Rate each of these frightening situations from one to ten, with ten being the greatest amount of fear that you'd experience:

_____ failing a test   _____ having no real friends

_____ staying alone in my home   _____ being without a boyfriend

_____ worrying about the future   _____ dealing with family problems

_____ losing someone I love   _____ facing serious health issues

Read Isaiah 41:13: *I am the Lord your God, who takes hold of your right hand and says to you, "Do not fear; I will help you."* What does God say about these scary, sometimes unavoidable situations?

_____

_____

_____

Read the verse in Isaiah again. Did you notice that during difficult times God takes *you* by the hand instead of the other way around? Like a loving parent, He senses danger just in time and grabs hold to ensure your safety. There's no letting go when the Father protects His daughter.

Even though you believe in God's caretaking skills, the uncertainty of tomorrow can sometimes overwhelm you: "What if I choose the wrong career? What if my dreams are unrealistic?" Read Deuteronomy 31:8 in your Bible. What does God say about the tendency to stress out over the future?

_____

_____

_____

Your Father knows what will happen tomorrow. In fact, He has already forged ahead to make sure that you'll be safe and protected. And when rough spots happen along the way, He promises to stay right with you. After all, that's what good parents do. Talk to Him now about the security of His protection.

Turn the page, and use the space provided
to tell God what's on your heart.

one more thing . . .

Many Christians memorize Jeremiah 29:11, a powerful verse claiming God's protection. Write what this verse means to you.

_____

_____

_____

_____

_____

_____

_____

_____

_____

_____

_____

_____

_____

_____

_____

_____

_____

_____

_____

_____

_____

_____

_____

_____

_____

_____

day 4: your Father forgives you.

Have you ever intentionally hurt someone? Did that person forgive you? Did you forgive yourself? We all know that God forgives sin. But how many of us believe that when we truly repent, He scoops us up and says, "Forget about it"? He's the kind of Father who doesn't hold grudges. Are you the kind of daughter who accepts His forgiveness?

When you've sincerely repented for a particular sin, how would you rate your lingering feelings of guilt or shame? Mark an "X" on the following line:

very ashamed   somewhat ashamed   a little ashamed   not ashamed at all

Hebrews 10:22 is one of my favorite verses dealing with God's forgiveness: *Let us draw near to God with a sincere heart in full assurance of faith, having our hearts sprinkled to cleanse us from a guilty conscience and having our bodies washed with pure water.* Look closely at the verse, and underline all the comforting phrases for daughters who disappoint their Father.

As far as God is concerned, it doesn't matter what you've done in the past. When you approach Him with an honest heart, He washes you clean of all that ugly sin. After that, let it go; God certainly has. Read 1 Peter 2:24.

1. Because of His sacrifice, how should you live?

_____

_____

_____

2. How have you been healed from the pain of sin?

_____

_____

_____

Your Heavenly Father could rightfully choose to punish your sins. He could also banish you from sight, ignoring your cries for mercy. But instead, He welcomes you back into His arms, rejoicing that you've come home. Spend some time asking for forgiveness of unconfessed sins. Then thank God for healing your wounds.

one more thing . . .

What does Psalm 103:12 say about God's "amnesia" when it comes to your forgiven sins?

_____

_____

_____

_____

_____

_____

_____

_____

_____

_____

_____

_____

_____

_____

_____

_____

_____

_____

_____

_____

_____

_____

_____

day 5: your Father gives great advice.

My dad has offered some wonderful advice during my lifetime: "Stay in school. That boy is not your type. Your car needs a tune-up." He isn't perfect, though, and neither am I.

Thankfully, however, the Heavenly Father makes no mistakes. Because He knows what's best, Jesus fully expects you to follow His advice. Read these words from John 10:27: *My sheep listen to my voice; I know them, and they follow me.*

I love the comforting words in this verse! First of all, Jesus proudly says that you, His child, belong to Him ("*my* sheep"). Secondly, He enjoys a personal relationship with you ("I *know* them"), even though He has many, many children. And because you love and respect your caring Father, what should you as His daughter do?

_____

_____

_____

When Jesus says "follow me," what are some specific ways that you can follow Him on a typical day? List them here, and then circle two ways that need more attention or emphasis in your everyday life.

_____

_____

_____

Read Proverbs 2:1–6 in your Bible. This passage is essentially a "cause and effect" message from God. After thinking on these verses, fill in the blanks below:

If you do this: _____

then this will happen: _____

Are you willing to trust the wisdom of your Heavenly Father? Talk with God about your need for guidance. Tell Him that you're open to the wisdom He offers. Then thank Him for being the Father who truly knows best.

one more thing . . .

James 1:5 is clear about what to do when you need solid, Biblical advice. Write the verse, and consider memorizing it.

_____

_____

_____

_____

_____

_____

_____

_____

_____

_____

_____

_____

_____

_____

_____

_____

_____

_____

_____

_____

_____

_____

_____

_____

Week 3

embracing true beauty

Several young Christian women recently discussed their struggles with growing up in today's world. Of the six concerns they mentioned, half dealt with insecurities. In their words, they aren't "good enough, pretty enough, or loved enough." Needless to say, these daughters suffer from a huge identity crisis! This week you'll see what God has to say about His treasured creation—you. You'll also discover ways to combat the negativity that threatens your God-given joy.

I praise You because I am fearfully and wonderfully made; Your works are wonderful, I know that full well. Psalm 139:14

day 1: appreciate God's handiwork.

Do you like yourself? Silly question, I guess, but many girls are uncomfortable revealing their positive traits. Let's take a minute to appreciate God's creative expertise:

1. List three positive things about your physical appearance:

_____

2. Write two things that you're good at doing:

_____

3. List one academic subject in which you excel:

_____

Read Colossians 3:15: *Let the peace of Christ rule in your hearts, since as members of one body you were called to peace. And be thankful.*

As a cherished member of the King's family, what two feelings should dominate your heart?

_____

_____

     Are you at peace with the body, mind, and talents that God gave you? Have you thanked Him recently for creating you? Many girls are so critical of themselves that I wonder if they're hurting God's feelings; after all, He formed them with such tenderness and care! The secret of accepting yourself lies in Colossians 3:15, the verse you've just read. If your heart is filled with peace and thankfulness, then there'll be no room for insecurity.

     When I was a teenager, a popular phrase stated, "God don't make no junk." When God created you, He was happy with the outcome. Shouldn't you be satisfied, too? Read Isaiah 32:17 in your Bible. If you are a righteous daughter of God, then what three traits will invade your personality?

_____

_____

_____

     Spend some time praising your Heavenly Father for His beautiful creation, you included. Then thank Him for providing the peace and contentment that every daughter can have.

one more thing . . .

Pray Psalm 139:14 as your own personal prayer to the Father. Write about the meaning of being "fearfully and wonderfully made."

_____

_____

_____

_____

_____

_____

_____

_____

_____

_____

_____

_____

_____

_____

_____

_____

_____

_____

_____

_____

_____

_____

_____

_____

_____

_____

_____

_____

_____

day 2: refute Satan's lies.

Satan would love for us to believe the lie of "not good enough." After all, when we are distracted by insecurities, our confidence suffers. This trick of Satan has deceived women since God's first daughter walked the earth. Is the same lie deceiving you? Look at 2 Corinthians 11:3: *I am afraid that just as Eve was deceived by the serpent's cunning, your minds may somehow be led astray from your sincere and pure devotion to Christ.*

From the verse above, can you see the danger in entertaining negative thoughts? Why does Satan want you to be distracted?

_____

_____

_____

The point is, of course, that Satan told Eve a life-altering lie, and she fell for it. Look at how her existence changed afterwards: She became self-conscious about her body; she felt ashamed of who she was, and she faced a life of continuous stress and disappointment. To put it literally, believing this lie was the death of her!

Let's look at some potentially life-altering lies that Satan wants God's modern-day daughters to believe. Place a check mark if you've ever been influenced by these deceptions:

——— I'm not smart enough.   ——— I'm a disappointment.

——— I'm a boring person.   ——— I have no real talent.

——— I'm not pretty.   ——— I'm a useless Christian.

Why might you believe such harmful lies, even for a minute? Read Colossians 3:2 in your Bible to find a better way to occupy your mind:

1. If you want freedom from negative thoughts, then what should you think about?

_____

_____

2. What are some specific thoughts to consider when insecurities creep into your mind?

_____

_____

Protect the Father's truth with everything you have. How? When Satan tries to distract you, confront the lie with scripture, combat deceit with prayer, and ignore the negative messages that Satan suggests. Thank God now for His truth. Then ask Him to help you, His precious daughter, embrace it.

Turn the page, and use the space provided
to tell God what's on your heart.

one more thing . . .

Read 2 Corinthians 10:5. List some negative thoughts that you need to "take captive." Then pray for God's strength in overcoming them.

_____

_____

_____

_____

_____

_____

_____

_____

_____

_____

_____

_____

_____

_____

_____

_____

_____

_____

_____

_____

_____

_____

_____

_____

_____

day 3: watch what you see.

I'll admit it: Sometimes when I'm channel surfing, the remote control pauses on an image of a beautiful celebrity. Within seconds, I'm comparing my imperfect body to one that's 50% plastic and 100% good lighting. Why do I torture myself? The feelings of frustration that follow are not Biblical, productive, or healthy. An old children's song warns, "Be careful, little eyes, what you see." King David said it another way in Psalm 101:3: *I will set before my eyes no vile thing.*

Does your self-esteem suffer when you look at potentially vile or hurtful things? Check any images that may negatively affect how you view your own body:

_____ magazine or billboard ads   _____ TV shows

_____ music videos   _____ girls around me

_____ movies   _____ internet sites

In what way can these images be harmful to you as a young woman? As a Christian?

_____

_____

_____

Psalm 141:8–10 clearly states where to focus your eyes. This passage also warns about possible danger. Read these verses, and then answer the following questions:

1. Where should your eyes be fixed?

_____

2. What is the advantage of keeping your eyes on God?

_____

3. If you keep your eyes on the Father, then what will happen?

_____

The threats listed in Psalm 141 are similar to advertisements targeted at today's teenagers. Everywhere you look, there's overwhelming pressure to be perfect. From hair products to skimpy clothes to diet pills, these marketing ploys suggest that physical beauty is the key to happiness. But it's not!

Verse nine is the perfect prayer to help you avoid the lies of false advertising: *Keep me from the snares they have laid for me, from the traps set by evildoers.* Today, thank God that physical perfection isn't His criterion for measuring your worth. Then ask the Father to protect your eyes from the snare of destructive images.

one more thing . . .

When looking at what Jesus faced during His time on earth, it seems shallow to get caught up in physical appearances. Read Hebrews 12:2–3, and talk to Him about the ultimate sacrifice.

_____

_____

_____

_____

_____

_____

_____

_____

_____

_____

_____

_____

_____

_____

_____

_____

_____

_____

_____

_____

_____

_____

_____

_____

_____

_____

_____

day 4: concentrate on inner beauty.

A local business advertises its "Full Day of Beauty," which is basically six hours of pampering. Clients are treated to manicures, haircuts, massages, and facials. Sounds luxurious, right? While there's nothing wrong with some physical upkeep, we all know that spiritual growth should take first priority. And ironically, the more time we devote to our inner selves, the more attractive our outer bodies seem.

Look at Peter's 2000-year-old advice to daughters just like you in 1 Peter 3:3–4: *Your beauty should not come from outward adornment, such as braided hair and the wearing of gold jewelry and fine clothes. Instead, it should be that of your inner self, the unfading beauty of a gentle and quiet spirit, which is of great worth in God's sight.*

1. Is there anything wrong with a stylish haircut or really cute jeans?

_____

2. What is Peter's point regarding your physical appearance?

_____

The last part of this verse explains how to become even more worthy to God. Oh, that His approval would matter the most! According to 1 Peter 3:3–4, what inner qualities are beautiful to God?

_____

_____

_____

Here's a tough question: How much time do you spend taking care of your physical body in relation to focusing on spiritual beauty? Mark your answer with an "X" on the graph below:

100% emphasis on   100% emphasis on
physical appearance   spiritual beauty

_____

As a woman who enjoys a new lipstick every now and then, may I offer some advice? Throughout the years, spiritual beauties have impressed me much more than the physical beauties I've known. Oh, I remember the Homecoming Queen, but her once-lovely face is now hazy in my mind.

Those who influenced my faith, however, are as clear as day: A friend who told me the truth when I didn't want to hear it; a cousin whose sense of humor cheered me up, and a paralyzed classmate who praised God with tears in his eyes. Ladies, that's real beauty. It comes from God, and it lasts forever.

Read the last half of 1 Samuel 16:7. Think about what's inside your heart. Confess any ugliness you might find there, and ask God to help you make inner beauty the top priority.

Turn the page, and use the space provided
to tell God what's on your heart.

one more thing . . .

Read Psalm 19:14 as your prayer for the day. Write it here:

_____

_____

_____

_____

_____

_____

_____

_____

_____

_____

_____

_____

_____

_____

_____

_____

_____

_____

_____

_____

_____

_____

_____

_____

_____

day 5: see your eternal value.

I've heard that the best way to raise self-esteem is to help other people. If you've ever visited a nursing home or taken food to the poor, then you understand this concept: At that humbling moment of giving to others, you suddenly understand your eternal purpose.

If you're a born-again daughter, then you possess specific traits that help others find Jesus. Read Galatians 5:22–23 in your Bible, and then list these traits, or fruits of the Spirit. Circle the qualities that describe your personal, God-given strengths:

_____

_____

These fruits of the spirit, along with the spiritual gifts mentioned in 1 Corinthians 12, are inside you for the sole purpose of leading others to God. Read 1 Peter 4:8–10: *Above all, love each other deeply, because love covers over a multitude of sins. Offer hospitality to one another without grumbling. Each one should use whatever gift he has received to serve others, faithfully administering God's grace in its various forms.*

1. Looking at the verse above, underline specific ways you should use your spiritual gifts.

2. List some specific instances when your spiritual gifts could be used to show God's love.

_____

_____

Why were you created in the first place? Your primary purpose is to praise God. You are also called to share Christ with others. How cool is that? Holy God entrusts you to lead other children into the Kingdom!

Do you realize your unique placement in God's plan? Spend some time thanking God for using you to do His important work. Then ask Him for wisdom in being a daughter of eternal significance.

one more thing . . .

Let's recap this week's focus on seeing yourself as God's worthy creation.

Day 1: Appreciate God's handiwork.
What do you like about yourself?

_____

_____

Day 2: Refute Satan's lies.
What lie has Satan told you? How will you combat his deception?

_____

_____

Day 3: Watch what you see.
When you feel insecure, where can you find acceptance?

_____

_____

Day 4: Concentrate on inner beauty.
Do you prioritize spiritual beauty over physical traits?

_____

_____

Day 5: See your eternal value.
What spiritual gifts are you using for God's glory?

_____

_____

week 4

protecting the name

My dad always took great pride in our family's last name. He often reminded me of its good reputation and of my role in keeping its integrity. After a talk like that, I was determined to keep my nose clean! As daughters of the Heavenly Father, your priorities should be similar. You are incredibly blessed to inherit the name *Christian,* and with this privilege comes great responsibility. Whatever you do and wherever you go, the name of God must be protected.

> *Be blameless and pure, children of God without fault in a crooked and depraved generation, in which you shine like stars in the universe, as you hold out the word of life.* Philippians 2:15–16a

day 1: know when to defend your faith.

I don't know about you, but I'm pretty defensive when someone criticizes my mother, my sister, or my dog. Do you feel the same way about your family? Are you just as protective with the name of your Christian Father? In what ways have you defended your faith?

_____

_____

_____

_____

_____

_____

_____

_____

_____

Almost everywhere you go these days, the Father's character is insulted. I'm guessing that you've noticed the blatant disrespect in television, movies, songs, etc. Let's look at a few ways that today's world misrepresents the character of God. Match the lies in the left column with the Bible's truth on the right.

1. Using God's name disrespectfully

    a) *They will turn their ears away from the truth. . . .*
       2 Timothy 4:4

2. Telling obscene jokes or stories

    b) *You shall not misuse the name of the Lord your God.*
       Exodus 20:7

3. Creating new religions opposed to God

    c) *Nor should there be coarse joking, which is out of place...*
       Ephesians 5:4

As a daughter of God, you must speak up when the family's reputation is threatened. Read John 2:15–16 in your Bible. Why did Jesus defend His Father's house?

_____

_____

Jesus showed righteous anger when the "family home" was disrespected. Of course, these "religious" moneychangers supposedly knew better than to ridicule God. Do the blasphemous people that you encounter know better? Talk with God about the chance to share God's love with those who distort His truth. Then thank your Father for the privilege of defending His holy name.

one more thing . . .

Some Christians have trouble defending their faith because they are either embarrassed or afraid of being rejected. What does 1 Peter 4:14 say about those who stand for Christ?

_____

_____

_____

_____

_____

_____

_____

_____

_____

_____

_____

_____

_____

_____

_____

_____

_____

_____

_____

_____

_____

_____

_____

_____

_____

_____

_____

day 2: know how to choose your words.

As a worthy daughter of Christ, you probably attend church regularly. You might even take your Bible to school, reading it in plain view. Chances are pretty good that a Christian T-shirt is in your closet, ready to be worn at a moment's notice. The point is, you're probably a walking advertisement for your beliefs. That's not a bad thing, I don't think. But keep in mind that if you're going to "walk the walk," then you'd better "talk the talk."

When you speak, do people associate you with sincerity and kindness? When you're telling a joke, expressing disappointment or talking about your day, do you sound like a daughter of God? One of the most effective ways to protect the name of Christ is with the use of your tongue. Read Ephesians 4:29: *Do not let any unwholesome talk come out of your mouths, but only what is helpful for building others up according to their needs, that it may benefit those who listen.*

I wonder what "unwholesome talk" might mean in 21st century terms. Make a list of things you may say which can undermine God's integrity:

_____

_____

It's probably no surprise that women are often accused of letting their mouths get them in trouble. In fact, the Bible is full of female disasters that began with foolish words: Jezebel's accusation of Elijah, Delilah's request of Samson, and Sapphira's lie to Peter, for example. Unlike these disobedient women, however, you must resist sinful impulses and allow the Holy Spirit to choose your words.

Controlling your tongue, an outward sign of Christian maturity, becomes critical when your words fall on unsaved ears. If your speech is no different from everyone else's, then how can you genuinely represent the Lord? Read Psalm 39:1 in your Bible.

1. When is it most important for you to monitor your words?

_____

_____

2. List several situations when your words can impact unsaved people.

_____

_____

_____

Proverbs 15:4 says, *The tongue that brings healing is a tree of life, but a deceitful tongue crushes the spirit.* With just a kind word, those who don't know Christ can experience true healing. The question is, are you ready for spiritually mature speech? Talk to God, first confessing the damage you may have done with your tongue. Then praise Him for giving you the Bible, His perfect, holy words.

Turn the page, and use the space provided
to tell God what's on your heart.

one more thing . . .

James 3: 2–5 discusses the power of honorable speech. Read these verses, asking the Holy Spirit to alert you *before* your tongue inflicts damage.

_____

_____

_____

_____

_____

_____

_____

_____

_____

_____

_____

_____

_____

_____

_____

_____

_____

_____

_____

_____

_____

_____

day 3: know what (and what not) to wear.

When I was a teenager, my father had the final say on which swimsuit I wore. Basically, if any part of my torso was showing, the suit was inappropriate. Now, please don't get the wrong idea: My intent was not to dress suggestively, embarrassing myself and those around me. I simply wanted to look pretty, dress in the latest style, and get a great tan.

Fortunately, my earthly dad knew my Heavenly Father, and the two of them kept a young, naïve girl on the right track. You see, they understood what my sixteen-year-old brain hadn't yet considered: What I wore on the outside spoke volumes about my inner beliefs. And like it or not, my choice of fashion was a clear reflection of my Christian name. Let's see what the Bible has to say about clothes. Read 1 Timothy 2:9: *I want women to dress modestly . . . not with braided hair or gold or pearls or expensive clothes, but with good deeds, appropriate for women who profess to worship God.*

I don't believe that the apostle Paul is telling women to literally abandon all cute hairstyles or pretty jewelry. What do you think he's saying about a Christian female's appearance?

_____

_____

Paul's words suggest several important points for young ladies to remember:
1. If you're not careful, then the way you dress/look will consume your time and money.
2. If you're not careful, then the way you dress/look will distract from your inner beauty.
3. If you're not careful, then the way you dress/look will attract the wrong kind of attention.

Do you agree or disagree with Paul's statements about women's dress? Give reasons for your feelings:

_____

_____

Please answer *true* or *false* for the following statements:
_____ 1. I can look stylish and still represent my Father with appropriate clothing.
_____ 2. I must wear tight or revealing clothes in order for boys to notice me.
_____ 3. Many girls wear revealing clothes because they are desperate for attention.

_____ 4. If I dress "sexy," then boys are more likely to make crude or indecent comments to me.

Did you find that only the second statement is false? Read 1 Corinthians 6:19–20 in your Bible. Why should you want to please the Lord with your wardrobe?

_____

_____

Wanting acceptance is a major part of the teenage struggle. Believe me, I know all about it. I also know about the rewards of pleasing God with "stylishly modest" clothes. Pray about the image you're projecting. Better yet, take God with you to your closet. Go through your wardrobe, asking Him for final approval. The results will change you, inside and out.

one more thing . . .

Matthew 5:28 shows young women the importance of dressing modestly. What are the possible consequences of dressing inappropriately?

_____

_____

_____

_____

_____

_____

_____

_____

_____

_____

_____

_____

_____

_____

_____

_____

_____

_____

_____

_____

_____

_____

_____

_____

_____

_____

_____

_____

day 4: know where to direct your steps.

Think about the following question that a teenager once asked me, and write your own response. She said, "I want to convince my wild friends to follow Christ, so is it okay to party with them? I'd be a great role model for God, since they could see me having fun without alcohol or drugs."

_____

_____

I wish I could see your reply! Hopefully, you have a logical answer that agrees with scripture. Yes, you should share Christ with nonbelievers, and doing so means associating with them. But hanging out at wild parties? Let's think about *where* Jesus shared His message with sinners. Read these statements, and circle the locations of each interaction:

1. Nicodemus comes to Jesus' dwelling at night asking for salvation. (John 3: 1–21)
2. An adulterous woman visits a well, where Jesus happens to be. (John 4: 6–42)
3. Another adulterous woman is brought to Jesus near the temple. (John 8: 3–11)
4. Jesus eats dinner at Matthew's home, along with tax-collecting sinners. (Matthew 9: 9–12)

Now check all the statements about Jesus' witnessing tactics that are true:

_____ Jesus used everyday places as opportunities to witness.

_____ Jesus was perfectly willing to be seen with sinners in public.

_____ Jesus visited sinners' homes in order to share the Gospel.

_____ Jesus hung out in evil places to influence people who were

actively sinning.

Did you mark all but the last statement? Even though Jesus talked to anyone who would listen, He always chose surroundings that were favorable to sharing His faith. Specifically, He never witnessed to people while the actual sins were being committed. Can you imagine Jesus explaining God's forgiveness while the taxpayers ran around stealing money? And while He had no problem talking with prostitutes in public, Jesus stayed away from the establishments where their sins took place. The same logic goes for you when it comes to hanging out in godless places. There is a time, but there is also a *place,* to share the gospel.

As a teenager, I stayed clear of sinful surroundings for a couple of reasons. One was to avoid unnecessary temptation. The other was a real fear of compromising my Christian integrity. And while my social life may have suffered temporarily, I knew that God would reward my convictions. Read 1 Corinthians 8:9 in your Bible. How does this verse apply to being in sinful situations with unsaved friends?

_____

_____

_____

God wants you to honor His name wherever you go. Pray for those who need a spiritual change of address. Then ask the Father to provide an opportunity for sharing His truth at the right time, in the right place.

Turn the page, and use the space provided
to tell God what's on your heart.

one more thing . . .

Make a list of unsaved friends that you see in everyday situations. Then commit to praying for opportunities to share Christ with them. You'll have answered prayers in no time!

_____

_____

_____

_____

_____

_____

_____

_____

_____

_____

_____

_____

_____

_____

_____

_____

_____

_____

_____

_____

_____

_____

_____

day 5: know why you work so hard.

Are you lazy? I don't mean the occasional "I'm going to sleep late on Saturday" kind of lazy. I'm referring to the habit of settling for mediocre. Whether you're washing the car or frying burgers for grumpy customers, do you settle for the least amount of effort? It's easy to do. And if you're not careful, the world will see your laziness and form negative opinions about God's family. For the Father's sake, when you have work to do, work very hard.

Read Ecclesiastes 9:10: *Whatever your hand finds to do, do it with all your might.* Regardless of the job you've been given to do, what should the quality of your work be?

_____

As a public school teacher for eighteen years, I often heard teachers complaining about students' poor performances. Sometimes, my heart ached to hear of a Christian student's laziness in class. More than once, these comments were made by unsaved teachers who, believe it or not, looked to their "religious" students as models of Christianity. Needless to say, an opportunity to show God's integrity was practically ruined.

Are there areas in your life that receive mediocre attention? Check any areas in which you have trouble giving your best effort:

—— eating healthy food   —— praising God   —— using time wisely

—— exercising   —— giving thanks   —— showing appreciation

—— doing homework   —— reading my Bible   —— showing respect

—— studying for tests   —— tithing   —— being punctual

—— helping with housework —— being organized   —— witnessing to friends

Sometimes, to be honest, I find myself suffering from laziness. What's strange is that I usually have no excuse for procrastinating: I've had enough sleep; the work is not too difficult, and the task can be completed within a few minutes. Yet, there I sit, a useless slug. Can you relate? All I can tell you is that God values hard work, regardless of your lazy mood. In fact, no matter what the job involves, there's a specific reason for doing your best. Read Colossians 3:17 in your Bible.

1. Why does Paul say to work hard?

_____

2. What does the verse say about your attitude while completing the task at hand?

It's time to praise God for the benefits of a job well done, talking with Him about the beauty of creation. Then praise the Father for all the reasons why you are able to do your best: your health, your bright mind, your goals, and your faith. Finally, ask Him to reveal where you need to work harder for the Family of God.

one more thing . . .

Consider memorizing Colossians 3:23, a short verse about working hard for the Lord. Then talk to God about giving your best.

_____

_____

_____

_____

_____

_____

_____

_____

_____

_____

_____

_____

_____

_____

_____

_____

_____

_____

_____

_____

_____

_____

_____

_____

week 5

managing emotions

How many emotions crowd your brain within a typical day? Four? Eight? Ninety-six? When I was a teenager, it seems that just one hour's time could mean the difference between excited jubilation and crushing disappointment. Is it just hormones? Is it an unavoidable part of the female experience? No matter how you feel, the Heavenly Father understands. Better yet, He empowers you through His Word and the Holy Spirit. Now *there's* a thought that evokes emotion!

> *The Lord, the Lord, is my strength and my song; He*
> *has become my salvation. With joy you will draw water*
> *from the wells of salvation.* Isaiah 12:2b-3

day 1: God helps you deal with disappointment.

Pretend for a minute that your entire life could be lived without any disappointment. You'd make an "A" on every math test; you'd always be the star of your team; no boyfriends would ever break up with you, and every new challenge would end in success. How do you like this daydream so far? Okay, now let's look at the downside of a perfect life on earth (yes, there are downsides). If you never experienced the pain of disappointment, then how would your spiritual life suffer?

1. Instead of leaning on your Heavenly Father for strength, you'd . . .

_____

2. Instead of learning from your mistakes, you'd . . .

_____

3. Instead of understanding the pain that others experience, you'd . . .

_____

_____

4. Instead of longing for the perfection of Heaven, you'd . . .

Even though disappointment is heartbreaking, these tough times are often faith-building experiences. When the hurt is fresh, though, how can you get past the pain? One way is to seek comfort in the promise of Romans 5:5: *Hope does not disappoint us, because God has poured out His love into our hearts by the Holy Spirit, who He has given us.*
According to this verse, what helps you cope with difficult experiences?

The Holy Spirit lives in you, providing hope and comfort during difficulty. He even prays for you when you're so saddened that the words just won't come. Read Romans 8:26 in your Bible. When you're especially distressed, how does the Holy Spirit help?

Praise God today for making you stronger through disappointment. Then thank Him for the Holy Spirit, who promises supernatural comfort in an imperfect world.

one more thing . . .

God understands your struggles. What does Isaiah 65:24 say about calling out to Him?

_____
_____
_____
_____
_____
_____
_____
_____
_____
_____
_____
_____
_____
_____
_____
_____
_____
_____
_____
_____
_____
_____
_____
_____
_____
_____
_____
_____
_____

day 2: God helps you manage anxiety.

When I was in high school, my mom used to say, "Treasure your teenaged years. This is the best time of your life." Best time? Was she kidding me? The stress of getting good grades, finding a boyfriend, and keeping my social status was enough to give me a nervous breakdown. If this was the climax of happiness, then I didn't want adulthood! Do you feel the pressure of your teenaged years? If you do, then the Heavenly Father offers a soothing remedy for His cherished, stressed-out daughter.

Have you talked with the Father about pressures in your life? List several things that often cause you stress:

_____

_____

Now read Psalm 55:22 aloud a few times if you dare, letting the words of God take on real power in your mind: *Cast your cares on the Lord, and He will sustain you; He will never let the righteous fall.*

Righteous daughters, your Father's shoulders are big enough to handle every crisis imaginable. In fact, when stress appears, He actually *wants* to take it away. So how can you surrender those anxious feelings and replace them with God's peace? Read Philippians 4:6–7 in your Bible, and then answer the questions below:

1. Every time you're anxious, what should you do?

_____

2. What should your attitude be when praying about anxiety?

_____

3. What should you expect after asking God to take away the stress?

_____

It is important to remember that even though God removes worry from your mind, He might not remove the source of anxiety: The coach may never treat you fairly; your boyfriend may dump you, and your parents may get on your nerves. But somehow, in the midst of the stress, you can feel an unbelievable calm.

Have you asked your Heavenly Father to take away the anxiety? Here are a few tips on how to escape the stress and feel the peace. Place a check beside those that you could try:

_____ 1. When praying about a problem, thank God in advance for taking away the stressful feelings.

_____ 2. Realize that the problem (not the stress) may hang on indefinitely. And that's okay. You'll simply learn to lean on God, even though life is temporarily tough.

_____ 3. Make a conscious effort to replace stressful thoughts with prayer, scripture, or praise songs.

_____ 4. Take good care of yourself: Get enough rest, eat right, and make time for some fun. Take a few minutes and think about the anxious thoughts that affect your life. Then, one by one, give these feelings to God, claiming His promise to give you peace.

Turn the page, and use the space provided
to tell God what's on your heart.

one more thing . . .

Write 1 Peter 5:7 here:

_____

_____

_____

_____

_____

_____

_____

_____

_____

_____

_____

_____

_____

_____

_____

_____

_____

_____

_____

_____

_____

_____

_____

day 3: God helps you squash jealousy.

Of all the feelings that I've experienced, jealousy is the one I most despise. Regardless of why I'm envious—and the list can be long—the emotion eats away at me, causing harm to myself and to the person I envy. God isn't so crazy about sinful jealousy, either. In fact, He says that it has no place in a Christian's life. Read James 3:14–15: *If you harbor bitter envy and selfish ambition in your hearts, do not boast about it or deny the truth. Such "wisdom" does not come down from heaven but is . . . unspiritual, of the devil.*

Where does envy come from?

_____

What an eye-opener! Anything from Satan has no use for God's daughter! So how can you shake the sin of envy? First, recognize what triggers these emotions. Check the areas that can "set off" the jealousy monster in you:

_____ another's good grades _____another's money _____ another's appearance

_____ another's family situation _____another's boyfriend _____another's personality

_____ another's material things _____another's social life _____ another's sprituality

Next, think about what happens when you entertain thoughts of jealousy:

1. How does jealousy affect your self-esteem?

_____

2. How does jealousy affect your relationships with others?

_____

3. Even if you keep these feelings to yourself, how does jealousy affect your relationship with Christ?

_____

Galatians 5:14–15 is clear about the destruction of letting jealousy creep into your emotions. Read the verse in your Bible, and then write the consequences of envy:

_____

_____

_____

Sister in Christ, there is no good reason to destroy yourself or another with jealousy. By the grace of your Father, you are a daughter of worth, destined for royalty in the palace of Heaven. That's more than you could ever ask for! Thank God, you have nothing—absolutely nothing—to be envious about.

Today, spend some time confessing any jealousy that distracts you from God's generosity. Then pray these words from Psalm 126:2–3, celebrating the blessings that *all* His children deserve: *Our mouths were filled with laughter, our tongues with songs of joy . . . The Lord has done great things for us, and we are filled with joy.*

one more thing . . .

Not all jealousy is from Satan. What does Exodus 20: 5 say about God's own jealousy?

_____

_____

_____

_____

_____

_____

_____

_____

_____

_____

_____

_____

_____

_____

_____

_____

_____

_____

_____

_____

_____

_____

_____

_____

day 4: God helps you clear up confusion.

Perhaps you looked at the title of today's devotion and thought, "I don't need to clear up any confusion. Everything is under control: social life, academics, future plans . . . nope, no uncertainty in my life." Well, hopefully this statement describes your sunny outlook, but I'm assuming you're like most teenaged girls who need a little help. The world is very confusing, even for "old-timers" like me! In order to be clear-headed, you have to look up.

What confuses you? Do relationships keep you puzzled? Is your future a source of bewilderment? If you feel any confusion, then explain it briefly here:

_____

_____

_____

The good news is that as a daughter of Christ, you can live confidently, without ever falling into the trap of confusion. You see, the Lord God is the Creator of clear thinking. Read 1 Corinthians 14:33: *God is not a God of confusion but of peace.*

1. If confusion is not from God, then where does it originate?

_____

2. Instead of feeling confused over a particular situation, what emotion does God provide for His children?

_____

When I finally realized that my feelings of confusion were Satan's tricks to, well, *confuse* me, I began to battle them with a few strategies. Check any of these that you might find helpful:

_____ 1. Spending frequent time with God is critical to keeping a clear perspective.

_____ 2. Trusting God for daily decisions is easier than figuring out His long-term plans.

_____ 3. "Nipping" temptation quickly keeps Satan from distorting God's clear voice.

When I need guidance for a confusing situation, one of my favorite verses is Isaiah 42:16. Read it in your Bible. In what way can this verse
provide reassurance when confusion overwhelms you?

_____

_____

God understands *exactly* how you feel during uncertain times.
The answers are unclear, and you don't know where to turn. But that's
all right because you're guided through the fog, one step at a time, by the
Creator of clarity.

Spend some time today thanking God for His guidance during
confusing times. Then trust His promise to lead you down a clear path.

Turn the page, and use the space provided
to tell God what's on your heart.

one more thing . . .

John 8:12 records the clear words of Jesus Christ to His followers. Read the verse, and then write about the optimism of these words.

_____

_____

_____

_____

_____

_____

_____

_____

_____

_____

_____

_____

_____

_____

_____

_____

_____

_____

_____

_____

_____

_____

_____

_____

_____

day 5: God celebrates your happiness.

I love to laugh. I'm not talking about polite chuckles but real, side-splitting belly laughs with the people I love most. For me, these moments are gifts from my Father who enjoys seeing me happy. Likewise, when you experience real fun, God celebrates the joy.

You've spent some time this week examining negative emotions that can affect you spiritually. But not all feelings are bad. When God created His daughters, He must have smiled at the silly, innocent things that make young women happy: cute puppies, warm brownies, and embarrassing situations that amuse you later. Being a girl has its advantages, and the ability to enjoy yourself is definitely a blessing.

How can you embrace happiness in a world filled with so much sorrow? Read Psalm 16:11: *You have made known to me the path of life; you will fill me with joy in your presence, with eternal pleasures at your right hand.*

One advantage of being God's child is an unshakeable, inner joy. After all, you have no reason for despair. According to the verse you just read, what will God make known to you, His joyful daughters?

_____

Because He takes great care of you, there is hope. And when you're hopeful, happiness isn't far behind. Psalm 16:11 says that you can be filled with _____ and with _____ . How's *that* for a reason to smile?

Surprisingly, I often meet unhappy Christians who claim to trust God, but their actions show doubt. They smile on the outside, but their hearts carry unnecessary burdens. These children of God are missing true peace and happiness. So laugh. Have a good time! And know that God directs all of your life, even those feelings of joy. Read Proverbs 17:22 in your Bible. What is the advantage of being a joyful Christian?

_____

Are you a happy daughter of Christ? I'm not suggesting that you'll never feel sad or discouraged. In fact, Ecclesiastes 3 states that you'll go through many emotions during your lifetime. But when the negative feelings descend, do you reach for God's inextinguishable joy? It's in you, you know. After all, you're His daughter.

Spend a few minutes praising God for all the happiness you experience. Thank Him for taking away the sorrows that have plagued you. Then ask your Father for help in embracing the genuine happiness that only He provides.

one more thing . . .

Read Psalm 18:19. Why has God rescued you from a life of sadness and sin?

_____

_____

_____

_____

_____

_____

_____

_____

_____

_____

_____

_____

_____

_____

_____

_____

_____

_____

_____

_____

_____

_____

_____

_____

week 6

choosing good friends

Few things are more precious to the female species than having friends. In fact, girls seem to travel in herds; have you noticed? They love to shop together, exercise together, and even visit the restroom together! Loyal friends, though, can be tough to find in a world so obsessed with selfish gain. This week focuses on the importance of friendship within God's family, whether you're looking for worthy friends or just trying to be one.

My command is this: Love each other as I have loved you. Greater love has no one than this, that he lay down his life for his friends.
John 15:12–13

day 1: a good friend is hard to find.

Having a trustworthy friend is huge, especially when you're a teenaged girl who needs to talk. Are you blessed with a Godly girlfriend who fits this description? I hope so. If you need a good friend, then I pray that God will send one your way. Why is it crucial for girls to choose best friends who have similar convictions?

A best friend is the person who's there when you want to:

  •Share your concerns, your disappointments, and your dreams

  •Have some fun

  •Grow spiritually as a daughter of Christ

This may sound melodramatic, but the people closest to you will either help or hinder your relationship with the Father. Read Romans 12: 9–11: *Love must be sincere. Hate what is evil; cling to what is good. Be devoted to one another in brotherly [sisterly] love. Honor one another above yourselves. Never be lacking in zeal, but keep your spiritual fervor, serving the Lord.*

After reading this passage about true love, describe the traits of a worthy best friend:

_____

_____

Let's look at a few examples of some spiritual giants and the company they kept: Who was David's best friend? A fellow believer named Jonathan. Who did Mary, Jesus' mother, confide in when learning of her glorious pregnancy? A Godly friend and relative named Elizabeth. Who were Jesus' closest confidants while He was on earth? His disciples, specifically Peter and John.

Having just one Christian friend is worth a thousand who don't share your beliefs. Read Proverbs 18:24. What is the advantage of one honorable friend?

_____

If you have a best friend who loves the Father, then thank God for this special gift. If you need friendship with a fellow sister in Christ, then talk with God about this particular concern. He'll help you find her sooner than you think.

one more thing . . .

Is Christian companionship important to your life? Read Genesis 2:18 for the answer.

_____

_____

_____

_____

_____

_____

_____

_____

_____

_____

_____

_____

_____

_____

_____

_____

_____

_____

_____

_____

_____

_____

_____

_____

_____

_____

_____

_____

_____

day 2: a good friend shares her faith.

On Day 1, we looked at the importance of treasuring Godly friends. If *all* your friends are Christians, though, then how will others see your faith? Through a quick smile as you walk past? By wearing a WWJD bracelet? This may be a start, but Jesus is clear about your role in reaching those who need Him. Read Matthew 9:12–13: *Jesus said, "It is not the healthy who need a doctor, but the sick. But go and learn what this means: I desire mercy, not sacrifice. For I have not come to call the righteous, but sinners."*

I'm sure you know several teenaged girls who are "sick" with sin. They need a Savior, and they need someone their own age—you—to help them meet the great physician. If you feel comfortable writing their first names, then do it here:

_____

Anyone can be *friendly* to a non-believer. But are you a *friend?* In order to show the love of Christ, you must establish relationships with those who need Him. Place a check beside any strategies that might reach the girls you've listed above:

_____ 1. Start a conversation about something non-threatening, like complimenting her clothes or discussing a class you have in common.

_____ 2. Invite her to do something that encourages conversation: working-out together, completing a school project, or trying out a new restaurant.

_____ 3. Spend time with her at your house, especially if your family is a Godly influence.

_____ 4. Invite her to a youth event at your church. Make sure that others treat her warmly.

_____ 5. Pray for opportunities to bond with her, so that she'll be open to your testimony.

Read 1 Peter 2:12 in your Bible. What is one way to influence non-Christian friends?

_____

According to this verse, "good deeds" are critical to reaching others. Years ago, a popular movie told the story of an outcast transferring into a particularly snobby school. Two of the main characters not only smiled at her, but they also begged, "Come hang with us!" And that's just what happened. This new acquaintance was invited to dinner and to visit their homes. She was treated as an equal by girls who hardly knew her.

No one is suggesting that you hang out exclusively with non-Christians, falling into their sinful habits. In fact, James 4:4 says that *friendship with the world is hatred toward God.* On the other hand, it's important to purposely seek out girls who need Christian friends. And then, according to scripture, you need to *be* one.

Do you need to expand your circle of friends? Pray for the girls around you who need Christ. If you can't think of any non-believing acquaintances, then ask God to open your eyes. He's waiting for a daughter like you to bring others into the Family.

Turn the page, and use the space provided
to tell God what's on your heart.

one more thing . . .

Are you nervous when talking with non-Christian friends about God? Read Exodus 4:12, and ask God to help you find the words.

_____

_____

_____

_____

_____

_____

_____

_____

_____

_____

_____

_____

_____

_____

_____

_____

_____

_____

_____

_____

_____

_____

_____

_____

_____

_____

_____

day 3: a good friend supports you.

I am blessed with friends who offer support without question. When someone is stressed, a great joke breaks the tension. If another has problems, all ears are listening. And after hearing good news, everyone celebrates! Christian support is vital in this frustrating world, and it's exactly what God expects of His daughters.

Let's see what Ecclesiastes 4:9–10 says about friendship: *Two are better than one, because they have a good return for their work: If one falls down, his friend can help him up.* According to the verse, why do you need supportive friends?

_____

As a female, you are naturally inclined toward being a good friend: You are especially skilled at communicating thoughts, and you understand emotions. You tend to nurture others, and you're probably a great listener.

1. Think of a time when you supported your Christian friends. Describe it briefly here:

_____

_____

_____

2. Now think of a time when your Christian friends supported you. Describe it briefly here:

_____

_____

_____

Being a true friend means that you focus on the traits listed in Philippians 2:1–2. Read these verses, and list some of the qualities of a Christian friend:

_____

_____

_____

Which traits describe you? Circle them (or ask your friend to circle them for you).

Sometimes it's difficult to offer support. Good friends can frustrate and anger you. They may reveal their unattractive sides, but God's commandment to love others remains constant. After all, that's what Christ does for you every day. 1 Peter 4:8 offers some great advice on support-ing each other, even when things aren't perfect: *Above all, love each other deeply, because love covers over a multitude of sins.* What does this verse say to you?

_____

_____

Pray specifically for your friends today, especially those who need support. Talk with God about these topics:

•Pray that your friends will feel comfortable and safe when confiding in you.

•Pray that you will love your friends, even when they aren't lovable.

•Pray that your friends will seek support in the ultimate friend, Jesus Christ.

one more thing . . .

Pray about re-connecting with a friend that you haven't seen in awhile.

_____

_____

_____

_____

_____

_____

_____

_____

_____

_____

_____

_____

_____

_____

_____

_____

_____

_____

_____

_____

_____

_____

_____

_____

_____

day 4: a good friend forgives and forgets.

Do you hold grudges? When a friend disappoints you, is it easy to forgive? Can you forget? Many friendships are permanently damaged, not by hurt feelings, but by unforgiving spirits. We all face specific challenges when close friends damage the relationship.

Check each situation that would be difficult for you to forgive:

_____ spreading lies about me   _____ telling lies to me

_____ sharing my secrets with others   _____ spending less time with me

_____ criticizing me   _____ not supporting my goals/dreams

These are some serious breaches of friendship! As far as I'm concerned, it would take the awesome power of God to change my heart from feelings of betrayal to forgiveness. Read Colossians 3:13: *Bear with each other and forgive whatever grievances you may have against one another. Forgive as the Lord forgave you.*

How is it possible to restore a broken friendship?

_____

_____

_____

Two truths stand out in this verse. One, the words "bear with each other" suggest that relationships involve mistakes committed by *both* parties. Second, the word "whatever" means that any grievance you marked in the columns above must be forgiven and forgotten. Yes, ladies, you must forgive just as God forgives you.

Read 1 Corinthians 13: 4–5. What does Paul say about remembering the times when your friends have hurt you?

_____

There should be no grudges, according to this verse, since dwelling on the pain will hurt everyone involved.

While God teaches you to forgive and move on, there are times when relationships may change forever. Please don't misunderstand me: Whenever possible, a good friend deserves every opportunity to remain close to your heart. But sometimes, even though you forgive and forget, it's best to distance yourself.

The Bible contains examples of moving on: Abraham and Lot went their separate ways after disputes over land. And the first missionaries, Paul and Barnabas, experienced some sort of disagreement that led to separate voyages during their ministries. Notice that there was no bitterness within the hearts of Abraham, Lot, Paul, or Barnabas. Each person forgave, forgot, and then moved on toward the Father's new direction.

God continually forgives and forgets your sins. Thank Him for His generosity. Then ask your Father for this same heart of mercy when your friends need forgiveness.

Turn the page, and use the space provided
to tell God what's on your heart.

one more thing . . .

Write Proverbs 17:17 here:

_____

_____

_____

_____

_____

_____

_____

_____

_____

_____

_____

_____

_____

_____

_____

_____

_____

_____

_____

_____

_____

_____

_____

_____

day 5: a good friend holds you accountable.

Let's pretend that your best friend, a committed Christian, begins "testing the waters" with some questionable behavior. She briefly mentions her recent activities, but you believe she's leaving out some sinful details. Do you challenge her apparent detour from the "straight and narrow"? Or do you wait silently, keeping your nose out of her business? Read Proverbs 27:6: *Wounds from a friend can be trusted, but an enemy multiplies kisses.*

1. Should you talk with your friend about her sin?_____

2. Why are you the best person for the job?_____

3. Are your words going to hurt her? _____

4. Is the truth better than lies from strangers?_____

Holding a friend accountable for her Christian walk is not just a choice but also a responsibility. Scripture is clear about helping friends turn back to God. Read Proverbs 15:31 in your Bible. Hopefully, what is the happy ending after you talk with friends about their sinful actions?

_____

If this situation ever occurs, let's hope that your friends will appreciate the wisdom of your words and turn back to God. In reality, though, they might be unwilling to consider the truth. If you've spoken to them in love, don't despair. Just pray that God will use your advice and your example to lead them back to Him. When confronting friends, 2 Timothy 4:2 explains exactly what to do and how do to it: *Preach the Word; be prepared in season and out of season; correct, rebuke and encourage—with great patience and careful instruction.*

1. Do these three things:

_____

2. Do them in these two ways:

_____

Have you ever been on the *receiving* end of some Godly advice? If so, then how did you take it? Unfortunately, the reaction is often anger, embarrassment, or hurt. But remember that Godly friends are commanded by the Lord to hold you accountable. Yes, it's uncomfortable, but the sting of accusation leads you back to the Father's arms.

Christian friends are placed in your life for many reasons, one being to strengthen your walk with Christ. Today, show your gratitude for God's plan. Thank Him for friends who hold you accountable, and then thank Him for the chance to help others stay true. Finally, thank the Father for giving you boldness and wisdom in guiding special friends back into the fold.

one more thing . . .

Galatians 5:7–8 is helpful when talking with Christian friends about their spiritual detours. Read it, considering this verse when counseling your "wayward" friends.

_____

_____

_____

_____

_____

_____

_____

_____

_____

_____

_____

_____

_____

_____

_____

_____

_____

_____

_____

_____

_____

_____

_____

_____

_____

_____

_____

_____

week 7

treasuring the family

As an Alabama native from a small town, I've been asked, "Who are your people?" This means, "Explain, in detail, your entire family tree." Let me ask you the same question: Who are *your* people? I'll bet you're thinking of relatives who are amusing, aggravating, disappointing, and supportive. And like it or not, they also influence your make-up. A scary thought? Well, relax. God has lovingly placed you with these specific people to fulfill a beautiful plan.

. . . I kneel before the Father, from whom His whole family in heaven and on earth derives its name. I pray that out of His glorious riches, He may strengthen you with power through His Spirit in your inner being, so that Christ may dwell in your hearts through faith. Ephesians 3:14–17

day 1: families sometimes struggle.

Regardless of how things may seem, every family sometimes struggles. Perhaps the problems are financial. Sickness may appear. Many families are torn right down the middle by the agony of divorce. Has your family ever struggled? If you feel comfortable doing so, then describe the experience here:

_____

_____

_____

Families in the Bible also endured tough times. The first family ever, Mr. and Mrs. Adam, suffered from communication problems (remember the "fruit incident"?) and eventually their son's murder. Job's family was successful one day and practically destroyed the next by financial loss and death. Since that time, countless families—maybe even yours—have lived through heartbreaks too painful to express.

So how can you remain hopeful when earthly families suffer? First, call upon the One who hears your cries. Read Jonah 2:2: *In my distress I called to the Lord, and He answered me. From the depths of the grave I called for help, and You listened to my cry.* Perhaps you can relate to Jonah's distress because you've been "swallowed up" by feelings of helplessness. But guess what? God isn't asking you to fix the struggle by yourself; He's just asking for a little trust.

If you've ever suffered through a family crisis and come out on the other side, then you can testify to the power of 1 Peter 1: 6–7. Read these verses in your Bible.

1. According to this passage, how long will your struggles last?

_____

2. According to this passage, what is the result of your trials?

_____

God loves your family, and He provides strength, regardless of the problems you face. Thank God for not only watching over you but also for getting personally involved with each crisis. Then give Him the glory for keeping your family strong.

one more thing . . .

Read 2 Corinthians 12:9–10. Why does Paul delight in the hardships that he endures?

_____

_____

_____

_____

_____

_____

_____

_____

_____

_____

_____

_____

_____

_____

_____

_____

_____

_____

_____

_____

_____

_____

_____

_____

_____

day 2: children must obey.

Did you notice the title of today's devotion? Did it rub you the wrong way? For a variety of reasons, obeying parents becomes especially difficult during the teenaged years. Oh, maybe you follow their wishes, but suddenly there's resentment about the boundaries. Or perhaps there's confusion over your parents' rationale in creating these rules. Everyone knows the Bible's stand on giving honor to parents. But can you do this with a willing heart?

Do you ever have trouble understanding the rules in your house? Mark any of these situations that describe your parents' priorities:

_____ setting a strict curfew   _____ demanding church attendance

_____ insisting on modest clothes   _____ enforcing rules about dating

_____ expecting excellent grades   _____ assigning household chores

Now that you've vented some frustrations, let's go to the Bible. Read Colossians 3:20: *Children, obey your parents in everything, for this pleases the Lord.*

1. According to this verse, what pleases the Lord?

_____

2. Are some rules more important than others to follow?

_____

As I'm sure you know, God expects obedience in *everything,* regardless of how you feel about the rules or the rule-givers. This can be a tough one, huh? No one ever said obedience was easy.

When I was a teenager, my parents were stricter than many of my friends' parents, and I was sometimes teased about the places I couldn't go. But even then, I reluctantly understood that my parents were looking out for me. They didn't enforce their rules to embarrass me or to show mistrust. They were just determined to raise a daughter who would find—and maintain—God's favor. Now, as an adult, I owe them for many of my blessings.

Read Proverbs 22:6 in your Bible. What is the huge responsibility that your parents have been given?

_____

_____

God has charged your parents with the task—and the honor—of protecting and preparing a daughter of Almighty God. He holds them personally accountable for you. In fact, one day they'll answer to God for all their decisions in raising each child. No *wonder* they want you home on time!

My prayer is that you will appreciate the daunting amount of love and responsibility behind your parents' decisions. Take some time to pray specifically for your mom and dad. Ask that they'll find the wisdom they need. Then commit yourself to obedience with a willing, respectful heart.

Turn the page, and use the space provided
to tell God what's on your heart.

one more thing . . .

Consider writing a letter of thanks to your parents for raising you, a worthy daughter.

_____

_____

_____

_____

_____

_____

_____

_____

_____

_____

_____

_____

_____

_____

_____

_____

_____

_____

_____

_____

_____

_____

_____

_____

day 3: parents make mistakes.

Around age sixteen, I realized that my mom was a person—a real, imperfect woman who was doing the best she could. My mother is a wonderful lady, and I'm blessed to have her in my life. But she makes mistakes, just like everyone else. Once I comprehended that my parents were, well, people, the easier it became to forgive their mistakes. Can you think of some ways that you've expected your own folks to be perfect?

I used to assume that my parents would always make good decisions. After all, they had tirelessly taught me right from wrong. And it was comforting, of course, to believe that intelligent adults were in charge of my well-being. But sometimes their human weaknesses appeared.

Have you seen it in your own folks? Perhaps they are short-tempered after a hectic day. Or maybe they show favoritism to your brother or sister. Sometimes parents *really* goof up and seriously affect the family long-term. Read 2 Corinthians 2:10–11: *If you forgive anyone, I also forgive him. And what I have forgiven—if there was anything to forgive—I have forgiven in the sight of Christ for your sake, in order that Satan might not outwit us. For we are not unaware of his schemes.*

In this passage, Paul speaks about the importance of forgiving good people who happen to make mistakes—people just like your mom and dad. Why is it important to forgive your parents when they are imperfect?

This passage is clear about Satan's plan to disrupt the family's peace. If the evil one convinces you to expect perfect parents, then he sets you up for conflict. You *must* ignore these lies of Satan and realize that when Mom and Dad mess up, it's because they are simply human. They deserve forgiveness, understanding, and another chance.

Perfect or not, good days or bad, you must strive to be a daughter of reverence. The honor you offer both parents is unconditional, regardless of your feelings or their mess-ups. Look at Deuteronomy 5:16. Write the first part of the verse here:

Are you an understanding, respectful daughter who honors her imperfect parents? If you struggle with forgiveness issues, then ask the Heavenly Father to gently change your heart. If you accept your parents, mistakes and all, then pray for them today. Finally, pray that you'll keep a tender, understanding heart for both Mom and Dad.

one more thing . . .

According to Luke 6:37, why should you always forgive your parents?

_____

_____

_____

_____

_____

_____

_____

_____

_____

_____

_____

_____

_____

_____

_____

_____

_____

_____

_____

_____

_____

_____

_____

_____

day 4: sibling relationships are complicated.

Not everyone is blessed with brothers or sisters who crowd the dinner table, borrow without asking, and specialize in aggravation. If you're an only child, read today's devotion with a heart toward your future college roommate or even your own kids someday. Everyone, I think, could use a word from God about close-knit relationships.

How is your relationship with each of your siblings? Generally speaking, how would you rate yourself on the "Sibling Meter"? Place an X on the line below:

---

very understanding/ loving	somewhat understanding/ loving	not understanding/ loving

Many issues can complicate your relationships with brothers and sisters. Check any of these situations that may describe your own family's conflicts:

_____ feeling jealous of a sibling

_____ believing that parents show favoritism toward a certain child

_____ trying to live up to a sibling's accomplishments

_____ forgiving a sibling who has caused pain within the family

_____ living in close quarters with siblings who have different interests

Read 1 Corinthians 1:10: *I appeal to you . . . in the name of our Lord Jesus Christ, that all of you agree with one another so that there may be no divisions among you and that you may be perfectly united in mind and thought.* How does this verse relate to problems with siblings?

One particular Bible story shows sibling love at its purest. Moses, leader of the Israelites, finds himself in the middle of an unusual battle. Whenever he raises his hands, the Israelites begin winning; when he drops his hands, the other tribe is victorious. Moses is exhausted. Then all of a sudden, his brother Aaron and brother-in-law Hur come to the rescue. Read Exodus 17:11–12 in your Bible.

1. How did Moses' brothers help him through a tough time?

---

2. From this story, what can you learn about supporting your
   own siblings?

_____

_____

Aaron could have been consumed with jealousy over his brother
Moses' achievements. After all, Aaron was the oldest sibling and commu-
nicated well, but stuttering Moses, the younger brother, became spokesman
for all of Israel. Aaron realized, though, what every believer must accept:
Regardless of circumstance, siblings support each other. Your brothers and/
or sisters need your unfailing love, in spite of what seems fair.

Today, praise God for the unique relationships you share with
your siblings. Then pray for them one by one, asking God to guide and
bless their lives.

one more thing . . .

If you have younger siblings, read 1 John 2:9. If you have older siblings, read Psalm 133:1. If you are an only child, read Romans 12:18, and then write a prayer for your family.

_____

_____

_____

_____

_____

_____

_____

_____

_____

_____

_____

_____

_____

_____

_____

_____

_____

_____

_____

_____

_____

_____

_____

_____

_____

_____

day 5: families bless us.

A friend of mine speaks fondly of her childhood. This may seem typical for most of us, but my friend suffered several tragedies early on. Her parents died, and the relatives who took her in were abusive. Her focus, however, centers on one grandmother who rescued her out of the pain and into a loving household. For my friend, the definition of "family" means an elderly lady in a tiny house. "My family is small," she says, "but I'm so blessed to have my grandmother."

Hopefully, your family is guided by Christian parents who lovingly set boundaries and joyfully embrace you. For many teenagers, though, supportive family relationships are found through church groups, distant relatives, or their friends' families. Wherever you find the love you need, these people are, by definition, your family. Today, let's celebrate them.

Read Psalm 33:11–12: *The plans of the Lord stand firm forever, the purposes of His heart through all generations. Blessed is the nation whose God is the Lord, the people He chose for His inheritance.*

1. If families follow God, then the plans of the Lord will
_____ _____ forever.

2. What happens to nations (or *families*) who make the Lord their God?

Families who follow God are blessed. In fact, you enjoy these blessings every day. Do you take time to thank God for them? Let's do so right now:

1. I know, without a doubt, that my family loves me because:

---

2. I have a good time with my family whenever:

---

3. My family has been financially blessed because we enjoy the luxuries of:

---

4. God answered my family's prayers when we needed His help in this way:

The key ingredient for successful families is found in 1 Corinthians 13:4–7, a familiar passage. Read it today as you think about your own family. Then list several Godly traits that should exist in your household.

_____

_____

_____

Godly families persevere. Despite your situation here on earth, worthy daughters enjoy an extensive Heavenly family with amazing heritage. The Father loves you, and He is so happy that you're His daughter! Tell Him how much you love Him, too.

Turn the page, and use the space provided
to tell God what's on your heart.

one more thing . . .

What can you do to improve the loving atmosphere of your home?

_____

_____

_____

_____

_____

_____

_____

_____

_____

_____

_____

_____

_____

_____

_____

_____

_____

_____

_____

_____

_____

_____

_____

_____

_____

week 8

dating with discretion

As far as boyfriends go, my teenaged years were uneventful. Guys who pursued me weren't my type, and guys I liked weren't interested. It wasn't easy, but I held onto God's promise of contentment, boyfriend or no boyfriend. My sisters in Christ, will you accept the Father's plan for your love life? Let's study the rewards and responsibilities of letting God be your matchmaker.

> *Discretion will protect you, and understanding will guard you. Wisdom will save you. . . . Proverbs 2:11–12a*

day 1: you can choose the right guy to date.

Several girlfriends during my teenaged years were, shall we say, perfectly willing to date questionable boys. From my perspective, these girls craved boyfriends strictly for social status—whatever *that* means—and frequently compromised their values as a result. In your opinion, why do some girls date boys who are obviously "wrong" for them?

_____

I hope you have a mental checklist for evaluating potential dates/boyfriends. Look at the list below, and mark all the standards you demand in a boy before dating him even *once:*

_____ commited relationship with Christ   _____ respect for his parents and family

_____ a desire for me to succeed   _____ health-conscious lifestyle

_____ genuine respect for my feelings   _____ confident and secure

_____ good reputation with teachers, etc.   _____ mature emotions

If you checked most of the items on the list, then your principles fit perfectly with the words of 2 Corinthians 7:1: *Since we have these prom-*

ises, dear friends, let us purify ourselves from everything that contaminates body and spirit, perfecting holiness out of reverence for God.

This verse describes the company you should keep—pure, holy, reverent believers—and that includes boys you date. A familiar verse, 2 Corinthians 6:14, is often mentioned when girls ask about dating non-Christians. In this passage, what instruction does God give His daughters?

_____

_____

Who you date (or don't date) will result in closeness with Christ or distance from Him. As you think about the criteria that your boyfriends must meet, answer these questions:

1. If you're dating for fun and not for a relationship, then does 2 Corinthians 6:14 still apply? Why or why not?

_____

_____

2. Are you willing to "settle" for a boy that does not meet all your standards? Why or why not?

_____

_____

3. If you haven't met a Godly guy, then are you willing to be "dateless" and happily single? Why or why not?

_____

_____

Today, think about the criteria listed above. Ask God to tattoo these on your brain. Then ask Him for wisdom in choosing the right kind of boy to date.

one more thing . . .

Should God have any say in whom you decide to date? Read Jeremiah 10:23.

_____

_____

_____

_____

_____

_____

_____

_____

_____

_____

_____

_____

_____

_____

_____

_____

_____

_____

_____

_____

_____

_____

_____

_____

_____

_____

_____

_____

day 2: you can insist that boys treat you well.

As a high school teacher, I have witnessed boys treating their girlfriends badly. Sometimes there was physical abuse. Other times, verbal insults or mean-spirited teasing was the weapon of choice. I counseled several young ladies whose boyfriends had "cheated" on them repeatedly. Each time, my heart broke to see beautiful girls who unnecessarily surrendered their self-esteem. Why do you think that girls date boys who treat them with disrespect?

_____

I've observed that girls allow boys to treat them badly for several reasons. One is a lack of positive male influences, and another is confusion over the definition of love. Read 1 Corinthians 13:6–7, looking for traits of healthy, Godly relationships: *Love is not rude, it is not self-seeking, it is not easily angered, it keeps no record of wrongs. Love does not delight in evil but rejoices with the truth. It always protects, always trusts, always hopes, always perseveres.*

1. If a boy cares for you, then he will *never*_____

2. If a boy cares for you, then he will *always* _____

As a daughter of worth, you should expect to be treated well. Dating the wrong guy is a tragic waste of *you*, God's beautiful potential. Read Matthew 7:6 in your Bible. What can this verse teach you about relationships with neglectful boys?

_____

Ladies, your priceless worth has been established by God Himself. Don't spend your energy and affection on boys who "trample you under their feet." A student once asked me if her boyfriend was treating her well enough. (Hint: If you have to ask that question, then the answer is "no.") Here is a test to determine whether or not a boy is worthy to date. Check any that you especially want to remember:

_____ 1. Boyfriends should always make you feel smart, funny, and pretty.
_____ 2. Boyfriends should always leave you with a clear conscience after the date is over.
_____ 3. Boyfriends should always be secure enough to let you spend time with your friends.
_____ 4. Boyfriends should draw you closer to God, encouraging your relationship with the Father.

_____ 5. Boyfriends should always make you feel good inside (not sick, worthless, jealous, or angry).

Many girls settle for boys who treat them badly. If you are one of these girls, then read today's study again, meditating on your worth in Christ. Then talk to someone—an adult—who can help you. If you are blessed with a healthy perspective, then thank God for the privilege of living as His treasured daughter. Finally, pray for those Christian sisters who, at this moment, are struggling over boys that they date.

Turn the page, and use the space provided
to tell God what's on your heart.

Ava H. Sturgeon

one more thing . . .

Be careful of boys who flatter you with manipulative words. What advice does Ephesians 5:6–7 offer?

_____
_____
_____
_____
_____
_____
_____
_____
_____
_____
_____
_____
_____
_____
_____
_____
_____
_____
_____
_____
_____
_____
_____

day 3: you can go too far.

Christian teenagers are typically interested in the topic of sex, primarily wondering where the line between innocent affection stops and sin starts. Some of them know the answer but hope that a new Biblical perspective will suddenly extend the boundaries! The funny thing is, God hasn't changed in two thousand years, and He's not going to tweak His convictions for the MTV generation. So what does God say about kissing and all that other stuff? Frankly speaking, how far is too far?

As most of us realize, the Bible is clear about single people remaining sexually pure. Unfortunately, though, recent years have called into question the technical meaning of "pure."

Let's go to the dictionary for an official definition: To be pure is to be "clean and untainted." So how physically involved can a Christian sister get and still be "clean"? Look at Ephesians 5:3: *Among you there must not be even a hint of sexual immorality, or of any kind of impurity. . . .*

According to Ephesians, there must not be even a _____ of sexual impurity in your life. These hints of immorality can materialize in various ways. Consider these:

1. Telling or listening to sexual jokes
2. Reading material that is sexual in nature
3. Listening to friends or acquaintances tell of their sexual experiences
4. Watching movies, television shows, or internet sites that glamorize sexual impurity

Did you notice that the list above does not involve direct sexual contact? God wants His daughters *completely* removed from sexual sin, so for absolute protection, you must engage in physical *and* mental abstinence.

God's word teaches that *all* sexual activities should occur within the confines of marriage. I've heard teenagers claim that doing "everything except actual intercourse" is okay. Here's the deal, holy daughters of Christ: If you're unmarried, *a lot* of sin can occur between the acts of holding hands and having "actual" sex. Read these verses in your Bible, and summarize them:

•1 Corinthians 6:13

•1 Corinthians 6:18–20

Do you realize that God has perfectly good reasons for wanting

His daughters to remain sexually pure? List several possible reasons for His high expectations:

_____

_____

_____

_____

Ask your Father for stubborn conviction in protecting your body and mind from sexual sin. Praise Him for His perfect plan of marriage and sex. Then thank Him for the rewards you'll reap from obeying the wise word of God.

one more thing . . .

Read 2 Timothy 2:22. What sorts of things should teenagers focus on?

_____

_____

_____

_____

_____

_____

_____

_____

_____

_____

_____

_____

_____

_____

_____

_____

_____

_____

_____

_____

_____

_____

_____

_____

_____

day 4: you can handle a difficult break-up.

My heart was broken during my eighteenth year, just before final exams. The pain was deep, and I still remember every detail of that night over twenty years ago. Yes, life goes on, and the sharp edges of this memory have dulled over time. But during the midst of a difficult break-up, the tears were real. And God was on the scene, waiting to dry them.

Have you lived through a break-up? If you haven't, count your blessings, and then save this study for future reference! If you've experienced heartbreak already, then list five adjectives that describe your feelings at the time:

_____

For me, the most frustrating part was figuring out what went wrong. The reality is, though, that you may never understand why certain relationships don't work. Maybe you're not supposed to figure it out. In faith, just lean on God and trust Him for the end results. Read Ecclesiastes 11:5: *As you do not know the path of the wind . . . so you cannot understand the work of God, the Maker of all things.*

No one is denying that break-ups are tough, but heartbreak makes you a stronger, more empathetic Christian.

1. What can you learn about God during painful times?

_____

2. What can you learn about yourself during painful times?

_____

3. What can you learn about your friends during painful times?

_____

After a break-up, I remember well-meaning friends and family telling me all sorts of things to try and cheer me up: "You're better off without him. I knew that you two wouldn't last. His new girlfriend is *way* uglier than you!" Needless to say, the best advice comes straight out of God's word. Read Psalm 119:147–148 in your Bible.

1. Why does the writer call out to God?

_____

2. Where does the writer find strength to make it through the day?

_____

When teenagers pour out their hearts over broken relationships, I understand the hurt. But one thing I know from experience is that God will bring you out of the sadness and into His hope. I also know that after some time has passed, when God's new plan is revealed, you will be grateful for the break-up. Sounds crazy, but it's true.

If you're hurting from a broken heart, then turn to God. He alone is the constant in your life, and your hope must remain in Him. If you've not experienced this kind of pain, then decide right now to stay strong in Christ, no matter what lies ahead. Spend some time today focusing on something other than your own immediate needs: Praise the Father for His unfailing love.

Turn the page, and use the space provided
to tell God what's on your heart.

one more thing . . .

The first sentence of Psalm 142:3 is comforting. Write it here:

_____

_____

_____

_____

_____

_____

_____

_____

_____

_____

_____

_____

_____

_____

_____

_____

_____

_____

_____

_____

_____

_____

_____

_____

day 5: you can enjoy being single.

Do you know girls who are miserable unless they have boyfriends? I've wanted to tell them, "There's more to life than dating some boy! What about your goals? What about your friends?" Sometimes I speak up, and sometimes I don't. But always I pray that my Christian sisters will realize that being alone can be a fulfilling, happy experience—really! The apostle Paul recognized the freedom of being single. Read 1 Corinthians 7:32: *I would like you to be free from concern. An unmarried man [woman] is concerned about the Lord's affairs—how he [she] can please the Lord.*

According to this verse, what are two advantages of being without a boyfriend?

1. _____

2. _____

There is something joyful about living with no strings attached, completely open to God's direction. If you're not waiting for a boyfriend's phone call or obsessing about your date on Friday, then there's room for other things—namely, quality time serving your Father. Think of some other advantages to being single:

_____

When I was a teenager, being alone seemed to fuel my irrational fears. I saw other girls with boyfriends and wondered why no guys noticed me: Maybe they were repulsed by my physical imperfections or weird personality quirks. Perhaps God was preparing me for a lifetime of loneliness in the remote regions of a third-world country!

Years later (and several boyfriends later, I might add), God showed me that "the single life" had actually strengthened my faith. And most importantly, He revealed that life is not about waiting around for circumstances to change. While you're hoping for something else, you can actually *enjoy* the waiting period. Read Philippians 4:11–13 in your Bible. How does this passage relate to girls who want boyfriends but don't have them?

_____

How would you feel if a boyfriend weren't part of God's plan—at least for the time being? Check the statements that would accurately reflect your feelings:

_____ 1. I will follow God's will for my life, regardless of the direction that He leads me.

_____ 2. I will find daily happiness, regardless of my circumstances, because God is in control.

_____ 3. I believe that God will send His peace and contentment during every situation.

_____ 4. Even if God wants me single for the rest of my life, I can be happy and fulfilled.

For your prayer time, focus on the list above. For those statements you checked, thank God for His wisdom. Then for those statements you weren't able to check, ask God for guidance. Tell Him about your worries, and ask the Father to give you joy despite the circumstances.

one more thing . . .

Today, pray for your future. Commit your body, mind, and spirit to the Holy Father, acknowledging the Lord's sacrifice in making you a worthwhile daughter.

_____

_____

_____

_____

_____

_____

_____

_____

_____

_____

_____

_____

_____

_____

_____

_____

_____

_____

_____

_____

_____

_____

_____

_____

_____

_____

week 9

finding God at school

Recently, a girl who is home schooled said to me, "I get lonely learning at home." At the same time, several girls attending public school discussed their challenging experiences. And how about the private school advantage? One teenager voiced several concerns about the Christian academy she attends. So how can a daughter of God, regardless of her school choice, handle the difficulties of education? Why, with the wisdom of her Father, of course.

> *The fear of the Lord is the beginning of knowledge, but
> fools despise wisdom and discipline.* Proverbs 1:7

day 1: academic expectations are high.

Do you feel pressured to earn good grades? Whether you're writing an English paper, studying for a biology test, or preparing for the SAT's, the quest for academic achievement can be stressful. Perhaps your parents demand A's, or maybe the drive comes from within, a powerful need for success. What should you do when expectations of excellence overwhelm you? Your Father has advice for this very situation. Read 1 Chronicles 28:20: *Be strong and courageous, and do the work. Do not be afraid or discouraged, for the Lord God, my God is with you. He will not fail you or forsake you. . . .*

In this verse, David speaks to his son Solomon about building a temple. This same advice works for God's daughters now. List three positive commands for those who are stressed:

Be _____ .

Be _____ .

Do the _____ .

First, you must be strong, relying on God's eternal presence.

121

Second, you must be courageous, even when the challenge is frightening. Third, you must be willing to work hard for academic success. Here's a tough question: Do you procrastinate or settle for mediocre work, and then still hope for an "A" on that paper or test? Why should God bless laziness? Work hard, be courageous, and God will reward your efforts.

As a lifetime "A" student, high school geometry was my first academic challenge. I remember studying regularly, hiring a tutor, and then earning a disappointing "C." Had God broken His promise to reward me? Absolutely not. He was simply molding my future by revealing several truths: I really needed to depend on God; I really needed to evaluate the pride in my heart; I really needed to avoid careers requiring math skills! After the sting of a bruised ego healed, I thanked God for those valuable lessons. He had helped me succeed in growing as a person, and believe it or not, I eventually made peace with that "C."

Read Micah 7:8. What is the encouragement for God's daughters who struggle with grades and still come up short?

The Father promises that although you may fall temporarily, He will never let you stay defeated. Thank God for your amazing capacity to learn new things. Then ask Him for the desire to learn, the ability to remember, and the grace to accept your best effort.

one more thing . . .

Read 2 Corinthians 4:8–9. How does this verse apply to those who struggle academically?

_____

_____

_____

_____

_____

_____

_____

_____

_____

_____

_____

_____

_____

_____

_____

_____

_____

_____

_____

_____

_____

_____

_____

_____

_____

_____

_____

day 2: extracurricular activities are stressful.

One morning during an English class I was teaching, an honors student cried when asked a simple grammar question. It didn't take long to realize that finding a prepositional phrase was *not* her only problem. As we talked outside the classroom, she unloaded a heavy burden of responsibilities: softball practice, cheerleading try-outs, student government activities, and babysitting her two-year-old brother! This fellow sister in Christ had finally broken under the pressure. Are you overwhelmed with extracurricular "stuff"?

Let's try some math. On an average day during the school year, what percentage of your time is spent on the following activities?

_____ classes/your school day   _____ extracurricular activities

_____ family time   _____ homework

_____ church functions   _____ time alone with God

How do you feel about the division of your time? Circle any activities that seem disproportionate. You know, teenagers become extremely busy for a variety of reasons. Perhaps they are happiest when interacting with others. Maybe they're building their college resumes. Or it's possible that they crave popularity. Whatever the reason, being too busy can rob you of your spiritual perspective. Read 1 Timothy 2:1–2: *I urge, then, first of all, that requests, prayers, intercession and thanksgiving be made for everyone . . . that we may live peaceful and quiet lives. . . .*

As a daughter of Christ, you must balance yourself, carving out time for peace and quiet. Maybe this means eliminating an activity altogether, or perhaps you must re-prioritize so that God's presence is acknowledged. List a couple of times during a typical day that you can set aside for God:

_____

When I taught school, my commute to work was a favorite time for prayer. I'd play a Christian CD, sing aloud, and chat with God. Another opportunity was between classes—just a quick praise under my breath. Then after dinner, I relaxed on the back porch with my Bible and journal. Oh, I treasured this end-of-the-day, untimed meeting with my Father!

Is it possible to pack your days with too many "fun and games"? Certainly. Does this mean that Christian daughters should eliminate all the extras? Of course not. Read Ecclesiastes 11:9. What should you do while you are young?

_____

_____

Having a joyful heart is a wonderful gift. Too many teenagers, though, are so caught up in the demands of numerous activities that their genuine happiness suffers. So does their spiritual peace. Talk to God for a few untimed minutes, praising Him for His goodness, and thanking Him for His blessings. Then ask the Father to help you keep a spirit of joy and peace.

Turn the page, and use the space provided
to tell God what's on your heart.

one more thing . . .

Write Psalm 46:10 here. Think on the meaning of this verse.

_____

_____

_____

_____

_____

_____

_____

_____

_____

_____

_____

_____

_____

_____

_____

_____

_____

_____

_____

_____

_____

_____

_____

_____

_____

day 3: teacher relationships are challenging.

Every teenager must adjust to a variety of authority figures: school teachers, church leaders, coaches, and employers. This fact is inspirational if you admire those in charge and frustrating if you struggle with others. How can teenagers cultivate a Christ-like relationship with adults who challenge their patience or respect?

When I think about my high school teachers, their distinct personalities were sometimes frustrating. One had no control over the class' behavior, and another knew very little about his subject matter. Yet, according to the Bible, I was to treat each teacher with unwavering honor. Read Ephesians 6:6–7: *Obey them not only to win their favor when their eye is on you, but like slaves of Christ, doing the will of God from your heart. Serve wholeheartedly, as if you were serving the Lord, not men. . . .*

This verse is full of instruction for teenagers who question the abilities, the intelligence, or the qualifications of those in charge. Let's look at the passage more closely:

1. What is the *wrong* motive for obeying adults who have
   authority over you?

---

2. What is the motivation for serving them respectfully?

Like it or not, you must honor those in charge with cheerful obedience. Because they are always right? No, not necessarily. But because they serve in places of authority, believers are to comply without complaint.

What if a teacher says something that opposes your Christian beliefs? First of all, never obey *immoral* instructions from authority figures—the Bible is clear on that. But what should you do when a science teacher asks you to "prove" the theory of evolution? How can you stay true to your faith while respecting a teacher's authority?

As a student, I answered controversial questions objectively, not promoting any godless theories, but showing I had studied the material. During these times, a Christ-like respect for my teacher was critical, since I wanted him to see God's loving—not argumentative—truth in me.

Read 2 Timothy 1:13–14. How can you ensure that your faith isn't compromised by a non-believing authority figure?

If you guard your heart, then God will prohibit any negative influence from non-believers. And who knows? You might even influence them through your attitude of genuine honor.

Spend some time praying for all those who have authority over you. Ask God to bless them. If you need forgiveness for being disrespectful in any way, then share your remorse with the Father. Ask God to give you an honorable, patient heart for all those in charge.

one more thing . . .

Read Matthew 7:1–2. How can this verse apply to those who have authority over you?

_____

_____

_____

_____

_____

_____

_____

_____

_____

_____

_____

_____

_____

_____

_____

_____

_____

_____

_____

_____

_____

_____

_____

_____

day 4: peer relationships are difficult.

Dealing with high schoolers your own age—whether in the class-room or in a church youth group—can be difficult. Blame it on insecurity, hormones, or immaturity, but some teenagers' personalities are, well, challenging. But as a Christian, you must treat everyone with respect. That's *everyone*—including the girl who stole your boyfriend or the guy who has no manners. So how can you learn to love everyone? Thankfully, God's word offers practical advice for daughters who need help with peer relationships. Read the verses below, and then answer the questions that follow:

Do not go about spreading slander among your people. Leviticus 19:16

Be kind and compassionate to one another, forgiving each other, just as in Christ, God forgave you. Ephesians 4:32

Anyone, then, who knows the good he ought to do and doesn't do it, sins. James 4:17

Am I now trying to win the approval of men or of God? Or am I trying to please men? If I were still trying to please men, I would not be a servant of Christ. Galatians 1:10

1. Which verse applies to each situation?
a) A girl is being made fun of, and you are silent in her defense.

_____

b) Your friends want you to accompany them to a raunchy movie.

_____

c) You tell a friend something hurtful but true about a classmate.

_____

d) A boy teases you, hurts your feelings, and then asks you to forgive him.

_____

2. Which verse is applicable to a situation you're facing right now? What is God's advice about handling this particular relationship?

_____

3. Of the four verses listed, which is hardest for you to obey? Why?

_____

_____

As a high school teacher, I observed two particular students handle awkward situations with the grace of God. On a daily basis, they set themselves apart from all the drama with quiet respect for those around them. They never preached their values obnoxiously, but they consistently demonstrated sincere kindness. And then when speaking up was necessary, their peers listened openly with genuine respect.

Read Matthew 5:16. What kind of attitude does God expect from you when dealing with other teens?

Today, ask forgiveness for any shortcomings in your relationships. Get specific. Ask for wisdom as you deal with other teenagers, and thank God for His timeless, perfect instruction.

Turn the page, and use the space provided
to tell God what's on your heart.

one more thing . . .

Make a list of people you need to forgive, and then consider offering them a fresh start.

_____

_____

_____

_____

_____

_____

_____

_____

_____

_____

_____

_____

_____

_____

_____

_____

_____

_____

_____

_____

_____

_____

_____

_____

day 5: God's presence is unmistakable.

Is God noticeably present at your school? If you attend a Christian school, then He's surely in your curriculum. If you're home schooled, then He's probably within the parents who instruct you. If you're at a public school, then He's in the Christian clubs meeting after hours. No matter where you're educated, God's presence cannot be contained. Hopefully, He's shining brightly in you. Read Philippians 2:14–16: *Do everything without complaining or arguing, so that you may become blameless and pure, children of God without fault in a crooked and depraved generation, in which you shine like stars in the universe, as you hold out the word of life. . . .*

The thought of Jesus Christ choosing *you* to reveal His presence is exciting! According to this verse, what are the steps to making God a visible force in your life?

1. Do everything without _____

or _____ .

2. Become _____

and _____ .

3. Shine like _____

in the universe (or in your particular school).

4. Hold out the _____ .

I am a product of public school, and even though God was not officially welcomed, I saw His presence daily. If you have a similar experience, then write your examples beside mine:

1. Christian teachers (They could not share God from the chalkboard, but His love and presence were in their classrooms.)

---

2. Christian friends (These were like-minded classmates from various churches who shared my devotion to Jesus.)

---

3. Christian clubs (This was an opportunity to share Christ within the very buildings where Jesus was supposedly unwelcomed.)

---

4. Myself (Not only was Jesus on my mind throughout the day in prayer, but I was also committed to showing His love to those around me.)

No matter where you go to school, God provides specific instructions for you to follow. Read Joshua 1:7, and list four things that demonstrate His presence in your life:

Pray that God will keep you strong, courageous, obedient, and unwavering in your commitment to Him. Then ask the Father to remain a powerful presence during your school day.

one more thing . . .

Joshua 1:5 is comforting when you feel alone at school. What does God promise?

_____

_____

_____

_____

_____

_____

_____

_____

_____

_____

_____

_____

_____

_____

_____

_____

_____

_____

_____

_____

_____

_____

_____

_____

_____

_____

_____

week 10

spreading the word

As a daughter of God, how should you honor the Heavenly family? Hopefully, you praise the Father with song. Surely you show love to others. But what is your primary role? After being adopted as a child of God, your significance in the Family is huge: You, worthy daughter, must share the good news of Christ. So get out there, and spread the word!

How can they preach unless they are sent? As it is written, "How beautiful are the feet of those who bring good news!" Romans 10:15

day 1: have a story to tell.

If I asked you to explain the meaning of "salvation," then you'd probably talk about God's merciful love. You might say that Christ's death is the only way to erase sin. Then you'd explain that Jesus' resurrection is the promise of eternal life. Do you have a story to tell? If you're not certain, then go to the back of this book, read "Are You God's Daughter?" and find out for sure. If you remember joining the Heavenly Family, then briefly describe the day you decided to become God's daughter:

_____

_____

The *minute* that you joined the Family, a transformation began. Deuteronomy 26:18 is a perfect description of the day when the "new you" was born: *The Lord has declared this day that you are His people, His treasured possession as He promised, and that you are to keep all His commands.*

1. On the day that you were born again, you became one of

   God's, _____ and you also became His

   _____ _____ .

137

2. Because you are now in the Family, you are to keep all of

God's _____ .

Since the day you became a "treasured possession" of the Father, how has your story grown? Are your journals full of answered prayers? Are you constantly amazed at God's blessings? If not, then perhaps it's time to expand the story. The initial experience of your salvation is awesome, to be sure, but the adventure with Christ continues. Read Acts 22:15–16.

This verse states your importance as a witness to all that you've seen and heard. What works of God have you seen and heard lately? Write the question that's asked at the beginning of verse 16:

_____

_____

If your personal growth with God has been stagnant, then ask forgiveness for wasting precious time. Recommit to following His will daily, obeying His commands and looking for opportunities to share the good news. Finally, pray for specific people who need their own stories with Jesus Christ.

one more thing . . .

Believers in Jesus possess something that everyone else lacks. Read 1 John 5:10, and tell Jesus all that's in your heart.

_____

_____

_____

_____

_____

_____

_____

_____

_____

_____

_____

_____

_____

_____

_____

_____

_____

_____

_____

_____

_____

_____

_____

_____

_____

day 2: keep your life clean.

During my teenaged years, I didn't drink, and smoking was never a temptation. There was no chance I'd consider having sex, and profanity was out of the question. Even at a young age, God had placed within me a desire to share Him with others. Nothing—not a curse word or even a quick appearance at a wild party—was going to damage my chances of sharing Christ. With God's help, I was determined to keep my life clean.

When you make the decision to live cleanly, what's your primary motivation? Place a check beside any determining factors, and then circle the biggest reason you stay out of trouble:

_____ punishment from parents   _____ friends who hold me accountable

_____ dangers of harmful activities _____ possibility of a damaged reputation

_____ fear of God's judgment   _____ damage to my Christian influence

Believers in the New Testament faced an enormous challenge when sharing their faith. Since they were from Jewish and Greek backgrounds, people around them were wary of the new term "Christian." Read 1 John 3:9: *No one who is born of God will continue to sin, because God's seed remains in Him; he cannot go on sinning, because he has been born of God.*

How did New Testament Christians separate themselves from the world?

_____

After accepting Christ, you begin to desire the clean heart that He provides. The verse you've just read means that Christians stop sinning *habitually* because they want to please God. According to the verse, why is deliberate, continued sin impossible for a believer?

_____

Sharing Christ is so much easier when you become a living testimony. Unsaved friends, out of the blue, have asked me to pray with them, saying, "You seem to have good connections with God. Would you talk to Him on my behalf?" Suddenly, a door is opened, and I can mention my faith. Colleagues notice the lack of profanity in my conversation and assume that Christianity is behind my "G-rated" vocabulary. Another door is opened, giving me a chance to tell the Savior's story.

To all of my squeaky-clean sisters out there, stay vigilant. Being separate means living cleanly in *every* area, as far as sin is concerned. What are some "everyday" sins that can hurt your witness as a teenaged Christian?

_____

Read James 1:21–22. What is the Bible's advice for Christians who foolishly believe that "clean living" is easy?

_____

Thank God for the Holy Spirit, who convicts and keeps you strong in the face of sin. Then ask God to help you be a pure, encouraging Christian to those who need a Savior. Finally, as James 1:21–22 says, decide to do just what the word of God advises—be clean!

Turn the page, and use the space provided
to tell God what's on your heart.

one more thing . . .

What does 2 Corinthians 5:17 say about leaving your sinful life behind?

_____

_____

_____

_____

_____

_____

_____

_____

_____

_____

_____

_____

_____

_____

_____

_____

_____

_____

_____

_____

_____

_____

day 3: continue to grow.

Let's say that you've trusted Christ as your Savior, lived a clean life, and shared Christ with one person. Good for you! If you remain at this same level of spiritual maturity, though, is God satisfied? A question like this calls for a verse like 2 John 1:9. Please read it in your Bible. What does John say about Christians who simply maintain their present lifestyles?

_____

As a child of God who wants to influence non-believers, you must grow spiritually. A growing Christian is enthusiastic, knowledgeable, and faithful. Let's face it: If you plan to reach others for Christ, then you must constantly dig a little deeper.

In which areas do you need spiritual growth? Rank these areas from 1–6, with 1 being the area where you need the most improvement and 6 where you need the least improvement:

_____ memorizing scripture   _____ defending my faith to others

_____ strengthening my prayer life   _____ finding ways to share Christ

_____ using my spiritual gifts   _____ learning the history of the Bible

    1. Which item listed above seems the least interesting for you? Why?

_____

    2. Even if this item seems a bit dull, how could this knowledge benefit you?

_____

    3. Which item listed above is particularly interesting to you? Why?

_____

In 1 Corinthians 3:2–3a, Paul warns Christians about existing in a state of spiritual immaturity: *I gave you milk, not solid food, for you were not yet ready for it. Indeed, you are still not ready. You are still worldly.*

Over the past year, has your knowledge of the Bible increased? Maybe it's time to advance from simple milk to the solid food of spiritual maturity. According to this verse, how can you tell when you're ready to grow?

_____

_____

_____

When you abandon worldly ways in search of spiritual maturity, then you're ready for some solid, spiritual food. Until then, God is frankly not going to trust you with the good stuff. What are some immature thoughts or actions that you could abandon in favor of spiritual growth?

Today, praise God for your amazing capacity to grow smarter and wiser. Thank Him for giving you the know-how to bring others to God. Then ask Him to help you mature into a daughter who enjoys solid, spiritual substance.

one more thing . . .

Galatians 2:20 is encouraging to those who seek spiritual maturity. Write a letter of thanks for the hope that you have.

_____

_____

_____

_____

_____

_____

_____

_____

_____

_____

_____

_____

_____

_____

_____

_____

_____

_____

_____

_____

_____

_____

_____

_____

_____

day 4: influence your younger sisters.

When church youth groups get together, there's a noticeable social division between younger and older teens. High school girls avoid middle school students, and twelfth graders barely tolerate "baby" freshmen. Some separation is understandable, since just one year makes a world of difference in a teenager's development. But being completely divided is a disservice to younger girls who need positive influences: They need their older Christian sisters.

Do you have regular contact with a younger girl? Maybe there's a little sister at your house, or perhaps a younger neighbor is close by. Within the church are lots of possibilities. Write several names of younger girls that you see on a regular basis:

When I was thirteen, two high school seniors at my church were perfect in my eyes. They dressed stylishly, dated Christian boys, and knew the word of God. But more than that, they talked to me—not just a polite "hi," but real conversations about school or clothes or the song we learned in choir. And I watched them closely, because you see, I wanted to be just like them! Without knowing it, they taught me that staying close to God was important, fulfilling, and very cool. Is there an older Christian sister who has influenced you? If so, write her name here:

Galatians 6:10 tells us to take care of our own families—in this case, our fellow sisters in Christ: *As we have opportunity, let us do good to all people, especially to those who belong to the family of believers.*

Think for a minute about ways you can influence the younger girls around you. What are some practical ways that you can show them the genuine love of Christ?

If you are serious about influencing others to follow Christ, then you must show genuine kindness to everyone—even selfish, whining, giggling girls who are irritating beyond belief! It doesn't take much to impact a younger sister. Sincere, one-on-one conversations are pure gold in their eyes, and compliments from an older, "wiser" teenager are monumental. Most importantly, living out your faith with integrity can change the direction of someone watching you closely.

Daughters of worth are commanded to help others in their spiritual walks. Read 1 Timothy 1:5. What should be your motive for influencing younger girls?

Today, pray for the younger sisters you see. Pray that their lives will be guided by God, and ask that your loving influence will be steady and significant.

Turn the page, and use the space provided
to tell God what's on your heart.

one more thing . . .

What advice does 1 Corinthians 8:9 offer about influencing younger girls?

_____

_____

_____

_____

_____

_____

_____

_____

_____

_____

_____

_____

_____

_____

_____

_____

_____

_____

_____

_____

_____

_____

_____

day 5: reach non-believers around you.

Since you've completed ten weeks of this Bible study, you probably live a pretty wholesome life. You pray, attend church, and treat people nicely. But how much time do you spend actively sharing Christ with others? Check any of these "witnessing tactics" that you regularly use:

_____ praying for specific non-believers   _____ bringing up God in conversation

_____ inviting non-believers to church   _____ giving money/time to missions

_____ treating non-believers kindly   _____ telling my story to non-believers

As a daughter of Christ, one of your most exciting responsibilities is introducing others to Jesus. Throughout the day, you should be listening to God's voice so closely that you recognize every whisper of opportunity. Read Acts 26:15–18 in your Bible, and then answer these questions:

1. Why did Jesus appear to Paul?

_____

2. Why did Jesus send Paul into the world?

_____

When Jesus speaks to Paul in this passage, the instructions also apply to you: A daughter of God must open the eyes of non-believers. So how can you accomplish this sometimes intimidating privilege? Well, the list at the top of the page is a good start. What are some other ways to share the love of Christ?

_____

When I was a teenager, I sometimes relied on my Godly lifestyle to do all the "spiritual talking" for me. By being kind and staying out of trouble, I figured that people would observe my admirable qualities and then rush to the church-house for salvation! It took me a while to understand that God wanted my *words* to match my *actions*—there were times when I needed to speak up. If telling people about Christ scares you a little, then read Acts 18:9–10a: *One night the Lord spoke to Paul in a vision: "Do not be afraid; keep on speaking, do not be silent. For I am with you. . . ."*

Having a few butterflies about sharing your faith is understandable, especially if you don't have much experience. Here are a few tips that will help:

    1. Take time daily to read God's word and pray. Your head and heart must be ready to share.

2. Pray about specific non-believers that you know, as well as an appropriate "opening line."
3. Speak from your heart. Tell, in your own words, how Jesus changed your life. You don't have to say everything at once. Sometimes you'll share a little at a time.
4. As you share, the Holy Spirit is praying for you. Trust in His ability to give you the words.

Spend some time getting your heart ready to share Christ. If you need forgiveness, then get that straight. If you need a renewed relationship with your Savior, then start now. Finally, begin praying for the non-believers that you will reach, and be ready to fulfill your purpose.

one more thing . . .

Write the names of three people with whom you'd like to share Christ. Then pray regularly for an obvious opportunity, and expect it to happen.

_____

_____

_____

_____

_____

_____

_____

_____

_____

_____

_____

_____

_____

_____

_____

_____

_____

_____

_____

_____

_____

_____

_____

_____

_____

_____

week 11

fulfilling your purpose

When I was sixteen, my daydreams included a journalism career and marriage to a Southern guy who loved camping. Little did I know that God had something else in mind, guiding me instead toward a teaching job and a St. Louis man who hated "roughing it." A bit different from my original plans, huh? So how can you discover the path that you should travel? It's really a matter of preparing, listening, and waiting for the Father to reveal His worthy plan.

> *Wisdom is supreme; therefore, get wisdom. . . . Esteem her, and she will exalt you; embrace her, and she will honor you. She will set a garland of grace on your head and present you with a crown of splendor.* Proverbs 4: 7–9

day 1: be ready to hear God's voice.

Have you ever heard the voice of God? I've often longed to witness a booming voice declaring, in no uncertain terms, the answer to a particular question. So far, this has never happened. Do you struggle with knowing God's direction for your life? It's really no mystery, since God has provided everything you need to understand His guiding words.

If you want to hear God's gentle prodding, then your heart and mind must consistently prepare for the "still, small voice."

1. What are some practical ways that you can stay ready for God's guidance?

_____

2. How can you hinder God's influence?

_____

Some people downplay the relevance of scripture in today's world, simply because it's an ancient document. But the word of God still breathes! Do you realize that most situations you encounter are addressed, in one way or another, within the Bible? As a daughter seeking the Father's advice, begin with His word. Read Joshua 1:8: *Do not let this Book of the Law depart from your mouth; meditate on it day and night, so that you may be careful to do everything written in it. Then you will be prosperous and successful.*

1. How often should you meditate on God's word?

---

2. What are the advantages of reading God's word?

Christians want to make wise choices, and knowing the Bible is one criterion. Prayer is another. Have you prayed about a big decision lately? Jesus was faced with choosing twelve disciples, a task that required divine wisdom. Read Luke 6:12–13, and describe how He received an answer from the Father:

What's the first step in understanding God's direction? Open the lines of communication through some serious prayer and Bible study. Take some time today to search the scriptures for God's guidance. Then talk to Him, pouring out your heart in humility, hope, and faith.

one more thing . . .

Read Philippians 1:9–10, my prayer for you, Christian sister. What kinds of answers do you need from the Father?

_____

_____

_____

_____

_____

_____

_____

_____

_____

_____

_____

_____

_____

_____

_____

_____

_____

_____

_____

_____

_____

_____

_____

_____

_____

_____

day 2: be sensitive to the Holy Spirit.

A teenaged girl was upset because her parents disapproved of a non-believing boyfriend. While her family suffered under the strain of this rebellion, she defended her relationship by calling it a "soul-winning" opportunity. Can you see the flaw in her logic? The Holy Spirit *never* asks us to disobey Biblical truth—in this case, honoring parents and dating Christians. Romans 8:9 explains the Holy Spirit's role in making good decisions: *You, however, are controlled not by the sinful nature but by the Spirit, if the Spirit of God lives in you. And if anyone does not have the Spirit of Christ, He does not belong to Christ.*

1. What is the guiding compass that influences a Christian's decisions?

_____

2. If sin influences your decisions, then what does this suggest?

_____

Since the Holy Spirit is present, will He help you with decisions like choosing a college or finding a Godly best friend? Certainly! Jesus promises that the Spirit's wisdom lives within us. Read John 14:26, and summarize Jesus' words to believers:

_____

When you focus on God, the Holy Spirit goes to work. These strategies are helpful when you're searching for the Spirit's voice. Check any that you find helpful in your own life:

_____ 1. After praying, be quiet and still for a period of time, listening for God's whisper.

_____ 2. The Spirit's voice is often a continuing conviction over a *lengthy* amount of time, instead of a passing emotion.

_____ 3. After believing that the Spirit is leading you down a certain path, pursue it with deliberate intention. Trust God to confirm your convictions, and ask Him to close doors if you've misunderstood His direction.

Have you ever prayed about a dilemma and then felt the Holy Spirit guide you toward a specific solution? If so, recount it briefly here:

_____

_____

_____

The role of the Holy Spirit is enormous in helping you make the right choices. You must decide to listen, wait, and act. Talk with God about His gift, the Holy Spirit, and then be still, experiencing the awesome power within you.

Turn the page, and use the space provided
to tell God what's on your heart.

one more thing . . .

Read Acts 16:6–8 to see how the Holy Spirit closed a door for Paul and his companions.

_____

_____

_____

_____

_____

_____

_____

_____

_____

_____

_____

_____

_____

_____

_____

_____

_____

_____

_____

_____

_____

_____

_____

_____

day 3: be prepared to wait on God.

The Bible is full of answered prayers that began with long waits: For centuries, the Israelites prayed for release from Egyptian bondage before Moses finally appeared. King David wanted to build a temple during his reign, but his son Solomon eventually completed the project. And of course, the birth of the Messiah was anticipated for thousands of years. God expected patience then, and He expects patience now. Sometimes, God makes you wait.

Have you prayed about a concern or question that is still unresolved? If so, write it here:

If you're actively seeking guidance through the Bible, prayer, and Godly advice, then rest assured that the Father hears you. For whatever reason, though, He hasn't solved your dilemma yet. Read David's thoughts about waiting on God in Psalm 40:1: *I waited patiently for the Lord; He turned to me and heard my cry.*

1. The third word of this verse—"patiently"—is tough to hear. Why do Christians have trouble waiting on God's plan to be revealed?

---

2. Just because God isn't granting your request doesn't mean He's ignoring your plea. What reassurance about unanswered prayer do you find in this verse?

The Lord hears your cries, and He loves you enough to do what's best, even if it means waiting. Are there experiences in your life when a decision to wait was actually a blessing in disguise?

When I was eighteen, I wanted a part-time job to supplement my freshman year at college. Before each interview I prayed, but no one was hiring. After two months of rejection, the message was clear: Wait! So I did. And guess what? Instead of working, my spare time was spent making Christian friends and finding a new church. Then when I returned to college for my sophomore year, a retailer called *me* out of the blue, offering the perfect job!

When the solutions to your difficulties are not addressed immediately, God is simply being a wise, attentive Father. Read Isaiah 30:18.

1. Describe the kind of Father who asks you to wait:

---

2. How can your relationship with God grow stronger through the process of waiting?

Because God is gracious and compassionate, those who trust His timing are truly blessed. Are you willing to accept God's plan on a "need to know" basis? This is, after all, the definition of faith. Praise God today for His infinite wisdom, and then thank Him for loving you enough to do what's best, even when you have to wait.

one more thing . . .

Every believer must wait for God's ultimate plan to be revealed.
Read Romans 8:18–19 for a preview of the eternal goal.

_____

_____

_____

_____

_____

_____

_____

_____

_____

_____

_____

_____

_____

_____

_____

_____

_____

_____

_____

_____

_____

_____

_____

_____

_____

day 4: be willing to accept "yes" or "no."

Many Biblical heroes endured difficult situations. If you are familiar with these stories, then circle the outcomes that were positive:

Joseph—sold into slavery by his brothers

Peter—frightened during a storm at sea

Paul—frustrated by a "thorn in the flesh"

Let's look at the facts: Joseph and Peter prayed for deliverance and were spared from their frightening ordeals. Paul, however, prayed for relief from his struggle, but God did not remove the "thorn." Why does God say "yes" to some requests and "no" to others? And more importantly, can you learn to serve God faithfully, no matter how your prayers are answered?

Read Philippians 2:13, and then answer *true* or *false* for the following statements: *It is God who works in you to will and to act according to His good purpose.*

_____ 1. God loves me more than I could ever imagine.

_____ 2. God knows what is best, even when I can't see the end result.

_____ 3. God's eternal glory is more important than my temporary happiness.

Did you answer "true" to all the statements? God has lovingly placed you in His mighty plan, but you have limited access to the whole picture. Wouldn't you rather trust someone with divine perspective, even if this means an occasional "no" to your human requests?

When Jesus was about to be crucified, He begged God for a way out. Here was the precious Savior dreading pain but eventually accepting God's plan with absolute faith. Read Luke 22:39–43, paying close attention to Jesus' attitude. How did He end His prayer?

_____

Look at verse 43. When you are in despair over a situation not turning out the way you planned, God provides comfort. What gave Jesus strength after His prayer of anguish?

_____

God provides the same reassurance when your prayers aren't answered in the way you'd hoped. He's promised never to leave you, even when the answer is "no."

Today, tell God your innermost desires, since He wants an open, intimate relationship with His daughter. But at the same time, prepare to accept the final outcome, believing that His perspective is perfect.

one more thing . . .

Write 1 Thessalonians 5:18 below, making it your prayer to God today.

_____

_____

_____

_____

_____

_____

_____

_____

_____

_____

_____

_____

_____

_____

_____

_____

_____

_____

_____

_____

_____

_____

_____

_____

_____

_____

_____

_____

day 5: be confident of God's involvement.

Is God is involved in your life? According to the Bible, He wants to be. But many Christians, while acknowledging God's presence, don't allow Him to direct their paths. Check any statements below that describe your hesitation to accept the Father's wisdom:

_____1. I worry about a problem for days before actually praying about the issue.

_____2. I pray about a problem but still continue to worry about it.

_____3. I pray for God to answer my concerns in very specific ways without considering His will.

_____4. I complain about a situation, even though I've asked God to use me in every circumstance.

_____5. I expect answers to my prayers, but I'm not actively seeking God every day.

Do you see yourself in any of these statements? You may have experienced *some* doubt, but hopefully, your faith continues to grow. The Bible is full of "confidence-boosters" for Christians who need a little assurance. Read these verses, and then answer the questions:

Trust in the Lord with all your heart, and lean not on your own understanding; in all your ways acknowledge Him, and He will make your paths straight. Proverbs 3:5–6

Take my yoke upon you and learn from me, for I am gentle and humble in heart, and you will find rest for your souls. For my yoke is easy and my burden is light. Matthew 11:29–30

We pray this in order that you may live a life worthy of the Lord and may please Him in every way: bearing fruit in every good work, growing in the knowledge of God, being strengthened with all power according to His glorious might so that you may have great endurance and patience, and joyfully giving thanks to the Father. . . . Colossians 1:10–12

1. What are you promised when circumstances seem too confusing to understand?

_____

2. What should you do when decisions weigh you down?

_____

3. What qualities are promised when you offer a worthy life to God?

_____

What's the best way to receive the Father's wisdom? It's simple: Accept His offer!

Refuse to entertain Satan's doubt; seek guidance through the Bible and prayer; find God in your present circumstances, and expect to land on your feet. Then one day, after years of trust, you will have a full history of victory because you followed the Father. Read Proverbs 31:26, and write the verse here as inspiration for your future testimony:

Pray today about any statements of doubt that you marked on the list at the beginning of this lesson. Confess any unbelief, and then thank God for His promise to direct your paths.

Turn the page, and use the space provided
to tell God what's on your heart.

one more thing . . .

Are you facing any decisions that need divine intervention? Write them below, noting today's date. Then when God steps in and gives you an answer, write the date again. In no time, your faith will be strengthened with answered prayers!

week 12

living with optimism

Over the past eleven weeks, you've studied the privileges and responsibilities of being worthy daughters. Hopefully, you better understand God's unfailing love, and you believe in the Father's purpose for your life. You are blessed, Christian sister, with a life overflowing with God's acceptance, forgiveness, and opportunity! During this final week, let's look at the importance of staying true to your roots, the inherited bloodline of Jesus Christ.

Adorn yourself with glory and splendor, and clothe yourself in honor and majesty. Job 40:10

day 1: give honor to God.

Let me ask a rather obvious question: Why, exactly, should you honor the Heavenly Father? Write a brief prayer of praise, telling God why you offer Him complete loyalty:

_____

If your prayer is similar to mine, then perhaps you mentioned these reasons to honor God:

- He created me; I belong to Him.
- He never changes.
- He sent His Son to save me.
- He corrects my mistakes.
- He provided the Bible to guide me.
- He has a plan for my life.
- He knows me individually.
- He's preparing a home for me in Heaven.

God deserves all the treasures of this world for Himself, but He lovingly shares these blessings with you! Read Ezekiel 34:26: *I will bless*

*them and the places surrounding my hill. I will send down showers in sea-
son; there will be showers of blessing.*

In this Old Testament passage, God promised to provide His
Hebrew children with a King and prosperous future. In the New Testament,
King Jesus provided the way for *every* believer to receive God's numerous
gifts. Thinking about your own life, list the first five blessings that come
to your mind:

Do you honor the Father of Blessings with your lifestyle? Read
Hebrews 13:18 in your Bible. As a daughter of Christ, what should be your
greatest desire?

Today, pray for the continued longing to honor God in every way.
Then tell Him all the ways He deserves your heartfelt devotion.

one more thing . . .

Sometimes God disciplines His wayward children. Read Proverbs 13:18. Why should you be grateful for correction?

_____

_____

_____

_____

_____

_____

_____

_____

_____

_____

_____

_____

_____

_____

_____

_____

_____

_____

_____

_____

_____

_____

_____

_____

_____

day 2: recognize the holiness of God.

My favorite hymn is "Holy, Holy, Holy." Several friends dislike its slow tempo, but I've always loved the majesty of the message. The words, taken from Revelation, remind me of the day when all creation will kneel before God's throne. Until then, the closest I'll get to bowing with other believers is through weekly church attendance. When your Sunday service rolls around, do you actively worship the holiness of God?

Church is a natural place to appreciate the holiness, or divine purity, of the Father. If you're not careful, though, the experience can become routine. Don't let a weekly habit ruin your opportunity to worship God's awe! If you overlook His holiness, then you miss the majesty, the power, and the promise. Read Psalm 99:9: *Exalt [praise] the Lord our God and worship at His holy mountain, for the Lord our God is holy.*

1. According to the verse, how should you worship the Lord?

_____

2. Think about your own attitude at church services. How could you improve the quality of your worship?

_____

Even though you probably experience God's holiness during your quiet time, church is where you can *always* praise His majesty. Check any of these strategies that help you worship:

_____ 1. I expect to encounter God's holiness in church *every* time, so I always experience it.
_____ 2. I sit near the front of the church so that I'm less distracted by others.
_____ 3. I think about song lyrics, so the words become my personal prayers to the Father.
_____ 4. I take notes during the sermon, so I'm more likely to comprehend God's holy word.

Daughters are called to praise their Father's holiness *every* day—not just on Sundays—and they are also expected to be holy themselves. Read 1 Peter 1:15–16 in your Bible.

1. Which areas of your life should be holy (pure)?

_____

2. Why should you, as a child of God, be holy?

_____

3. Does a lifetime of "holy living" appeal to you?
Why or why not?

_____

_____

As a worthy daughter, being holy is both challenging and reward-ing. You may not be perfect every time, but working toward purity is all that God asks. Don't be frightened by a lifestyle of holiness; after all, the Holy Spirit is in you, making all things possible. Praise God for His pres-ence, and most of all, acknowledge His awesome holiness.

Turn the page, and use the space provided
to tell God what's on your heart.

one more thing . . .

Because you are holy, how should you spend your time? Read 2 Timothy 1:8–9.

_____

_____

_____

_____

_____

_____

_____

_____

_____

_____

_____

_____

_____

_____

_____

_____

_____

_____

_____

_____

_____

_____

_____

_____

_____

_____

day 3: receive happiness from God.

Let's begin today's study with a personal survey in the form of a true/false test:

_____ 1. I am generally a happy person.

_____ 2. I am usually content with my day-to-day behavior.

_____ 3. I maintain a pleasant attitude, even when circumstances are bleak.

_____ 4. I find that spending time with God gives me a peaceful outlook.

_____ 5. I want genuine joy so that people will see Christ in me.

Are you aware that real joy is possible right here on this sinful, imperfect planet? If you're taking advantage of God's promises, then you answered "true" for each survey statement. If you could use a little more happiness, then read Psalm 68:3 for some words of encouragement: *May the righteous be glad and rejoice before God; may they be happy and joyful.*

1. Who can gladly stand, without doubt or shame, before God?

_____

2. How should you feel about your day-to-day life here on earth?

_____

If you're not careful, then lots of daily irritations can spoil your God-given happiness. My particular challenge occurs early in the morning when the alarm clock sounds. How can I be happy when I'm running late and my clothes need ironing? Well, a continual, deeper joy keeps me calm, since the Father's eternal peace overpowers any temporary nuisances.

You can live majestically, with the happiness of God, even when times are tough. Habakkuk 3:17–19 offers a helpful dose of Biblical optimism. Find this verse in your Bible, and then answer these questions:

1. Even though circumstances seem bad, what can God's children do?

_____

2. With the strength of the Lord within you, what great things can you accomplish?

_____

Daughters of God, your lasting happiness is guaranteed, thanks to a supernatural strength you can always access. Isn't that a great reason to feel joyful?

Think of a time when you felt God's joy and contentment despite a tough situation:

_____

_____

I remember when two best friends turned their backs on God to pursue sinful lifestyles. Where did that leave me, odd-girl-out, when weekends rolled around? For a while, I sat at home alone, strangely content to watch reruns on cable and write in my journal. Depressing? Not really, because God had provided His obedient daughter with real, unexplainable peace.

Today, praise God for His guaranteed happiness, telling Him about the joys in your life. Finally, ask Him to remind you of the contentment He has promised His children.

one more thing . . .

James 5:13 offers advice for daughters who need some happiness. What does this verse suggest?

_____

_____

_____

_____

_____

_____

_____

_____

_____

_____

_____

_____

_____

_____

_____

_____

_____

_____

_____

_____

_____

_____

_____

_____

_____

_____

_____

_____

_____

_____

day 4: rest in the hope of God.

The modern definition of "hope" has changed a bit since the Bible was written. For example, when I hope that a purse goes on sale, I'm really wishing—not expecting—for the price to drop. When Job or David or Paul talked about hope, though, they believed that something would definitely happen—it was only a question of when. Ladies, you have the certain hope of Christ in you. How's *that* for optimism?

Verses dealing with hope are some of my favorite passages in the Bible, perhaps because they're so, well, *hopeful!* We could all use some confirmation of God's dependability every now and then. Read Paul's words of hope in Romans 5:5. *Hope does not disappoint us, because God has poured out His love into our hearts by the Holy Spirit, whom He has given us.*

1. According to this verse, hope does not ———————you.

2. How does your heart become full of God's hope?

When you're having a bad day, what does God promise? When you're lonely and need a friend, where is your hope? Here's some good news: God has promised to lovingly place His hope in your heart. Just hold on. God's hope does not disappoint.

What can you, as a believer, be hopeful about? Here are some areas that can be approached with Christian confidence:

•God has a plan for you.
•God provides you comfort during difficult times.
•God gives you spiritual gifts to use for His glory.
•God promises you eternal life.

Even when you're tired or confused, the Heavenly Father promises hopeful assurance. Expect it, and then accept it. Read a famous passage on hope, Isaiah 40:31, in your Bible.

What happens to those who hope in the Lord?

The Heavenly Father wants you to surrender every worry, letting Him provide hope instead. Will you tell Him today about the concerns on your mind? Ask forgiveness for bearing the burdens alone, and then give it all to Him. Begin to see that God's hope is a promise, not simply a wish. Then end today's prayer by thanking Him for the precious gift of certainty.

one more thing . . .

Hebrews 6:19 says that hope is an _____ for the soul. In what areas of your life do you see God's steady hope?

_____

_____

_____

_____

_____

_____

_____

_____

_____

_____

_____

_____

_____

_____

_____

_____

_____

_____

_____

_____

_____

_____

_____

_____

_____

_____

day 5: look forward to Heaven with God.

This is our last day together, worthy daughters, so let's spend it in excited expectation of our ultimate home. Do you ever dream about the day when you'll see Heaven for the first time? Are there specific Christian sisters that you can't wait to see? List some women that you plan to visit after entering those pearly gates, as well as the topics of conversation that you might suggest:

Here's my short list of saints that I hope to corner for some "girl talk," along with the questions I'd ask:

1. Eve—"How did it feel, those first few days, to be completely sinless?"
2. Lottie Moon—"What was it like to be an early, single, female missionary in China?"
3. Mattie Murphy—"Great-grandmother, do you realize the Godly legacy that you left behind?"

The older I get, the more exciting Heaven becomes to me. Maybe it's because each passing year means that more acquaintances will transition to their eternal home. Or perhaps it's because, as time goes on, I'm more aware of this world's imperfections. How do you feel about your eventual place of residence?

When your days on earth are difficult, you can lean on the promise of eternal joy. Read Philippians 3:20–21: *Our citizenship is in Heaven. And we eagerly await a Savior from there, the Lord Jesus Christ, who, by the power that enables Him to bring everything under His control, will transform our lowly bodies so that they will be like His glorious body.*

Don't you like the part about having a "glorious body"? I'm so excited! Seriously, though, some real truths appear in these verses that you need to embrace:

1. I do not belong here on this earth. My citizenship is in

    _____ .

2. I _____ await my Savior's return.

3. My Lord has the power to bring everything in this sinful world under _____ .

The majestic King is on the throne, and He'll return when it's time. Read Revelation 7:17 in your Bible. What is comforting about this verse?

_____

As a woman who cries at the drop of a hat, I'm looking forward to dry eyes! Peter must have felt the same sort of anticipation when he wrote this in 2 Peter 3:13: *In keeping with His promise we are looking forward to a new Heaven and a new earth, the home of righteousness.*

Today, pray with one purpose in mind, praise. Praise the Father for providing an eternal home, a reward that believers don't even deserve. Then praise your God for the many worthy Christian sisters who'll be in Heaven, standing with you.

Turn the page, and use the space provided
to tell God what's on your heart.

one more thing . . .

When your earthly body seems to shut down, don't worry. Read 2 Corinthians 5:1. What does God say about our "eternal house"?

_____

_____

_____

_____

_____

_____

_____

_____

_____

_____

_____

_____

_____

_____

_____

_____

_____

_____

_____

_____

_____

_____

_____

_____

_____

_____

are you God's daughter?

Can you know for sure that you belong to God? According to the Bible, you can be absolutely certain! More than anything, God wants to claim you as His treasured daughter. It's your choice, though, whether or not you decide to join the Family. It's not an automatic membership: You're not born into the family; you're not accepted just because you go to church, and you can't join simply because you're a good person.

Becoming a daughter of God is a deliberate decision to believe in Jesus and follow His teachings. Here's why: God sent His son Jesus to earth around 2,000 years ago and even though He was entirely human for 33 years, Jesus lived a perfect life. He didn't deserve to die, but sinners like you and me crucified Him. This was part of God's plan, since this perfect sacrifice was the payment for your sins. Three days later Jesus arose from the dead, proving that He was not only human but also fully divine.

When you believe in Jesus' death and resurrection and consciously decide to follow Him, then you inherit membership into the Family of God. If you haven't yet made this life-changing commitment, then tell God about your desire to join the family. Ask Him to forgive your sins; thank Jesus for dying in your place, and then express your desire to follow Him forever. That's all it takes!

If you'd like more information on becoming a daughter of God, then talk with your pastor or youth director. I'd also love to help, so feel free to e-mail me at avasturge@yahoo.com. May God bless you, fellow sister in Christ!

Here are some scriptures that explain how to join the Family of God:

God so loved the world that He gave His one and only Son,
that whoever believes in Him shall not die but have eternal life.
John 3:16

All have sinned and fallen short of the glory of God, and are
justified freely by His grace through the redemption that came by
Christ Jesus. Roman 3:23

Everyone who calls on the name of the Lord will be saved.
Romans 10:13

leader's guide

before the study begins

Thank you for offering to facilitate a teenaged girls' Bible study! Your influence and guidance will reap eternal benefits to future wives, mothers, and career women. Enjoy yourself, and expect to be blessed beyond measure. Here are a few preparations to complete before the study actually begins:

1. Publicize *A Daughter's Worth* several weeks before the first session is scheduled. Although the study is written primarily for high school girls who attend church, don't hesitate to market it as an outreach opportunity—the language is intentionally written for all types of backgrounds.

2. Order enough books for every participant. Students will use their own personal copies of the books, taking them home each week to complete the interactive devotions. At the end of the study, they will keep their books, filled with journal entries and Biblical truth, for future reference.

3. Decide on the length of each session. For the actual discussion each week, 45 minutes to one hour is probably sufficient. Extra time for fellowship and prayer, though, needs to be considered.

4. Calculate how many students your group can accommodate. If more than twenty enroll, you might consider meeting with everyone initially for an opening session and then breaking into smaller groups for prayer requests and more intimate discussions.

5. Plan on completing each devotion yourself, along with the participants, so that you can easily facilitate discussion.

6. Begin praying for each student who will join your study. Ask that God will prepare her heart, as well as yours.

during the first session

week 1/overview: recognizing your worth

The first session with your students will set the tone for the rest of the study. Aim for an environment that is comfortable, safe, friendly, and fun. Playing "cool" Christian music as students arrive is always a good idea, and refreshments would be welcomed. Many teenagers prefer sitting on the floor, so you might have throw pillows handy. Whatever you decide, your excitement and sincerity in meeting them will make the most impact.

1. Greet students warmly. Consider nametags and an ice-breaker. Introduce yourself, telling a bit about your passion for teaching this study.

2. Pass around an information sheet so that students can write their names, addresses, phone numbers, and e-mail addresses. Keep this information for future outreach and encouragement.

3. Distribute *A Daughter's Worth* books, asking each girl to write her name inside the front cover. Explain that this is her personal copy to take home, to write in, and to bring each week to the Bible study.

4. Introduce the Bible study by asking students to tell you the toughest parts of being a teenaged girl. Write their responses on a chalkboard or poster board so that everyone can see. Use the list as a springboard for several discussion questions:

a) Say, "Which item on the list is particularly tough for you?" Ask for a show of hands for each item listed.

b) Say, "Why is _____ so tough for teenagers?" (Choose an item on the list.)

c) Say, "How can a Christian teenager deal with _____ _____?" (Choose an item on the list.)

5. Ask students to open their books to the Table of Contents and glance at specific topics for the next twelve weeks. Point out any items on their "hardship" list that appear in the Table of Contents. Ask students which week/topic that they look forward to discussing most.

6. Turn to the Week 1/Overview page, "Recognizing Your Worth."

a) Ask students to read the first paragraph silently and then to answer the survey that follows. Discuss their responses to the survey.

b) Read Psalm 106:45 (verse is provided in the paragraph that follows the survey). Answer questions 1–2 aloud with students, giving them time to write their answers.

c) Ask, "How do you know that you're priceless to God?" Wait for answers. Then have someone read Romans 5:6–8 in her Bible. Fill in the last blank of the Overview together, using the scripture to answer the question.

d) Read aloud the last paragraph of the Overview that begins with "That's what this Bible study is all about. . . ." Encourage girls to follow through with the study.

e) Explain the section called *What to do Next . . .* so that students understand which devotions to complete for next week, as well as any supplies that they'll need.

f) Ask for prayer requests. If a teen is comfortable praying aloud, then let her volunteer. If not, then girls may pray silently or you may close the session in prayer.

for the remaining sessions

The purpose of each weekly session is to discuss specific topics in depth, prompting questions and giving students a chance to learn from each other (and from you). These suggestions will keep each session's format fresh and exciting:

1. You may occasionally facilitate each week's topic by discussing devotions one through five in order, pointing out central truths and using just a few of the questions to prompt discussion. Always refer to scriptures during the discussion so that any advice or instruction is based on God's truth alone.

2. You may begin the session by asking students which devotions were particularly meaningful for them, and start the discussion there. Be flexible, knowing that a lengthy discussion on one topic can be as important as short discussions covering all the daily devotions.

3. After a few weeks, you may ask for student volunteers to lead discussions on particular devotions for the following week. Students probably need specific directions for the first couple of times ("Find three key points in the devotion, and try to think of a personal example"), but eventually they'll be able to freely discuss a topic in depth. By the end of the study, you may very well assign every devotion for the week, realizing, of course, that you'll need to supplement or gently re-direct the discussion when necessary.

4. Look for contemporary props to encourage conversation. For example, Week 3's discussion on *Embracing True Beauty* could come alive with visuals like Barbie Dolls or (conservative) fashion magazines. Or for Week 7's *Treasuring the Family*, students could bring in some of their favorite family photos.

5. Feel free to ask a guest speaker to share briefly on the topic of the week. For example, a college student whose "love life" is above reproach could share on Week 8's *Dating with Discretion*. Just be sure that the speaker leaves time for students to discuss their thoughts.

6. Share a few of your own teenaged experiences so that students comprehend your empathy. Obviously, choose appropriate stories that are brief and relatable to their experiences.

7. Take time each week for prayer requests, and encourage students to record other girls' requests in the margins of their books. You might also provide index cards for students to write private prayer concerns for your eyes only.

tips for a successful study

1. Encourage students to complete all five devotions each week. Moreover, stress the importance of pacing themselves with just one devotion per day, rather than cramming all the devotions into one hour's time.

2. Realize that some students might not be God's daughters because they haven't yet placed their faith in Jesus Christ. During some point in the study, you might want to point out a section of this book called *"Are You God's Daughter?"* which is a brief explanation of salvation.

3. Tell students that you're praying for them by name every day. Then do it.

4. Teenaged girls' conversations can digress pretty quickly, turning a meaningful discussion into a gossip fest or random diatribe. Keep this in mind, being ready to "nip" it with humor and gentle cajoling.

5. Assure students that each weekly session is a safe place to ask questions, vent frustration, or reveal problems. Make an effort to speak with each girl every week, and encourage students to write their private prayer requests on index cards that only you will see. Then occasionally write them back with a letter in the mail, an e-mail, or a phone call. They *love* that!

6. Sometimes you may hear of serious issues like abuse that need immediate attention. You must report any discussions of this type to your youth director, minister, or government agency.

7. Look forward to spending time with God's girls. They are so hungry for mature, Godly women to show genuine interest in their lives. They will love you, and you will love them, too.

TATE PUBLISHING, LLC

Tate Publishing is committed to excellence in the publishing industry. Our staff of highly trained professionals—editors, graphic designers, and marketing personnel—work together to produce the very finest book products available. The company reflects in every aspect the philosophy established by the founders based on Psalms 68:11, "The Lord gave the word and great was the company of those who published it."

If you would like further information, please call
1.888.361.9473
or visit our website at
www.tatepublishing.com

Tate Publishing LLC
127 E. Trade Center Terrace
Mustang, Oklahoma 73064 USA

CPSIA information can be obtained
at www.ICGtesting.com
Printed in the USA
LVOW08s0711081116
512053LV00025BA/523/P